All My Days

by Ellen Mainville

Unless otherwise indicated, all Scripture quotations are taken from the Holy Bible, New Living Translation, copyright © 1996, 2004, 2007, 2013, 2015 by Tyndale House Foundation. Used by permission of Tyndale House Publishers, Inc., Carol Stream, Illinois 60188. All rights reserved. Some Scripture quotations from The Authorized (King James) Version - indicated by (KJV). Rights in the Authorized Version in the United Kingdom are vested in the Crown. Reproduced by permission of the Crown's patentee, Cambridge University Press.

Cover and interior designs by Ann Carlson Publishing.
Back cover scripture quotation: KJV.

Cover photo and artist photo © Andrew Mainville, Wenatchee, WA. Used with permission.

ISBN: 978-0-9962883-1-6

Library of Congress Control Number: 2017944660

Published in the United States of America

Ann Carlson Publishing
Malone, New York

www.threeoranges.net

Always my best friend,
my husband, Mark,
sons, Nate and Andrew
and Coco, who barks
Danielle and Heather
and my sister, Ann
all who inspire me
like no one else can

CONTENTS

LIST OF ILLUSTRATIONS

ALL MY DAYS

ALL MY DAYS

Psalm 23:6 "Surely goodness and mercy shall follow me all the days of my life, and I will dwell in the house of the Lord forever." (KJV)

Psalm 27:4 "The one thing I ask of the Lord - the thing I seek most - is to live in the house of the Lord all the days of my life, delighting in the Lord's perfections and meditating in his Temple."

Psalm 139:16 "You saw me before I was born. Every day of my life was recorded in your book. Every moment was laid out before a single day had passed."

All the days of my life contain a divine spark...the presence of God that infuses even the most ordinary moment with the breath of the miraculous. I am not always aware that he is with me. My mind is often clogged with the tasks at hand, the routine of the day, the work of living...but I have a longing to see God and to know that he sees me. When I do pause to open up my eyes to him, I see the traces of his love and protection scattered like manna upon the groundwork of my day. He is with me, giving me what I need to sustain me in moments of need, weakness, loneliness, heartache, sorrow and also joy, celebration and achievement.

God is with me; he never leaves me. Not a day goes by without his fingerprints upon it. No night drifts into darkness without the light of God illuminating a path before me. He goes ahead of me and he follows behind me. He is with me, not because of anything I have done, but because of who he is and the divine love he alone is able to give. Even though I do not always admit it, my heart yearns everyday for his unquenchable love. I need him.

"What can I offer the Lord for all he has done for me? I will lift up the cup of salvation and praise the Lord's name for saving me" (Psalm 116:12). So to the God who saved me and keeps me everyday in the hollow of his hand, I offer my praise and thanksgiving in these pages from my journals. I honor his presence in my home, his work in my heart and his guidance in my journey.

God is with me, all the days of my life.

GOD IN MY HOME

TO EVERY GENERATION

God in My Home

Psalm 119:90-91

"Your faithfulness extends to every generation,

as enduring as the earth you created.

Your regulations remain true to this day,

for everything serves your plans."

My home...the heart of everyday life beats within these walls. Here God meets me and causes me to grow in wisdom and understanding, so I know who I am and who he is. At the kitchen table God and I have conversations that no one else will hear, and there are sometimes tears and laughter that no one else will see...but everyday it changes me.

I come to God at my best, and I come at my worst...he is always there. He does not reject me or condemn me, but he speaks with me as my Father and helps me to understand, from ordinary things, the extraordinary power he holds and the intricate details he unfolds as he works in my life.

God uses moments in my day like colored snapshots to draw me back. "Look again," he says, "And see me." I look a little deeper, and there he is. I do my best and reach out to him having done all my "possible," and he reaches his hand down to me holding the "impossible." My life is infused with grace. The ordinary door of my home opens into the extraordinary realm of the heavens, and God is with me...in this house today.

WHEN PLAYFULNESS SLEEPS

BOY'S ROOM

Matthew 19:14 "...Jesus said, 'Let the children come to me. Don't stop them! For the Kingdom of Heaven belongs to those who are like these children.'"

Psalm 127:3 "Children are a gift from the Lord; they are a reward from him."

There's a room in my house
where dinosaurs walk
big ones and small ones
that giggle and squawk

Chaos reigns in that room
always in uproar
romping and stomping
that shakes every door

but when lights are turned down
and playfulness sleeps
my heart sees two boys
that innocence keeps

How can it be that those
reckless in daylight
now seem so fragile
so gentle and slight

The softness of night and the innocence of sleep change everything. I look at the faces of my sleeping children and forgive them everything that went amiss in the reckless abandon of play. I see them as they are: fragile, transient, innocent...precious beyond words. The dark eyelashes sweeping round cheeks, lips delicate as rose petals, damp curls framing the face...my heart melts. I wish that I could wake them to say the "I love you" that was forgotten in the chaos of the day. But that moment is gone forever and my heart cries, "Please God, let me remember to say it tomorrow." I kiss the sleeping cheeks, feeling the gentle puff of warm breath on my own cheek, and I know I am rich beyond measure and blessed, but also fragile and vulnerable in my humanity. "How can I do this, God?

How can I raise these children you've given me?"

But God is there with me; he reaches down and kisses my cheek and whispers in my heart the "I love you" that he never forgets to say. He holds my hand and tells me, "We'll do it together. I'll help you. I am with you always."

God is With Us

Isaiah 41:10 "Don't be afraid, for I am with you. Don't be discouraged, for I am your God. I will strengthen you and help you. I will hold you up with my victorious right hand."

Joshua 1:9 "...Do not be afraid or discouraged. For the Lord your God is with you wherever you go."

Matthew 28:20 "...And be sure of this: I am with you always, even to the end of the age."

Zephaniah 3:17 "For the Lord your God is living among you. He is a mighty savior. He will take delight in you with gladness. With his love, he will calm all your fears. He will rejoice over you with joyful songs."

God is with me
    in this house today
  he is at my side
   offering grace and strength
    to do whatever I must do
God is with me
   waiting with words of comfort and peace
   listening
     though I do not speak
God is with me
   in this house today
but I live the day
   shouldering so many impossible things
   for me to bear alone
  as if God were far away
   on some distant glorious hill
    watching but never touching
   the ordinariness of my day
blinded eyes have read the word
  and never seen that
    God is with me

The ordinary days are often the days that defeat me. The repeated tasks wear grooves in my spirit...a sore spot of frustration and boredom. I wonder, "Why? What can be accomplished by so many trivial things?"

But God is with me. He is in this house today. God is present, infusing every thought, every task, every moment with divine presence and purpose. My life, the work that my hands find to do, the words that I speak, the lives that I touch, these are not trivial things to God. God is with me...in this house today.

CROSS STITCH

*Psalm 139:13-16 "You made all the delicate inner parts of my body and knit me
together in my mother's womb. Thank you for making me so wonderfully complex!
Your workmanship is marvelous - how well I know it. You watched me as I was being
formed in utter seclusion, as I was woven together in the dark of the womb. You saw
me before I was born. Everyday of my life was recorded in your book. Every moment
was laid out before a single day had passed."*

*Galatians 2:20 "My old self has been crucified with Christ. It is no longer I who live,
but Christ lives in me. So I live in this earthly body by trusting in the son of God, who
loved me and gave himself for me."*

> Stitch stitch stitch
>   I sew up the fabrics and colors of my day
>   red tent on sea foam carpet
>   orange and black caterpillar in a green coffee can
>   pink watermelon
>   tawny sand
>   little boy blues
>
> Stitch stitch stitch
>   sometimes the threads are even and precise
>   and sometimes I tangle
>   and knot them under the fabric of the day
>   as I hurriedly sew this imprint of life
>   confined in a hoop of hours
>
> Stitch stitch stitch
>   a pattern emerges
>   but I am only half the design
>   the pull of my single stitch pale and incomplete
>   until it is covered by the cross.

Sitting at night with my thread and hoop and needle, I create a silken replica
of life. Flowers, bees, watermelons entwined in their vines....all are beautiful and
intricate and complicated and at times frustrating and maddening as the threads
twist and I lose my count and must begin again. But the result, as beautiful as it

is, would not be possible if each stitch was not covered by its cross. One single stitch does not produce a color vibrant enough or a texture rich enough. The stitch must first be laid down, and then it must be covered by the cross, which falls back over it and makes it complete. As I carefully work each stitch, I can not help but see the parallel between my needlework and the reality of my life and my need for the cross. The cross of Jesus Christ must fall upon everything; it must cover everything. Without the cross, without the sacrifice of Christ's blood which redeems me, the pattern and purpose of my life is frail and incomplete.

THE PERFECT DAY

Psalm 103:13-14 "The Lord is like a father to his children, tender and compassionate to those who fear him. For he knows how weak we are; he remembers we are only dust."

Lamentations 3:22-23 "The faithful love of the Lord never ends! His mercies never cease. Great is his faithfulness; his mercies begin afresh each morning."

Deep down in my soul
    I set my heart on having the perfect life
  children never argue
    they love to shop for groceries
no one gets a headache
    no one's hair sticks up straight in the morning
      children don't get wiggly and complain when they have to sit still
When it doesn't happen each day
  I am disappointed
    maybe not much
      but still
    just a little bit disappointed
I sulk
  and don't enjoy the brief moment
    when a child slides a warm hand into mine and smiles
  I miss the rainbow on the wall that dances
    as the sun hits a dirty drinking glass in the sink
    I miss the music
      in bare feet running down the hall
My father God doesn't miss such things
  he is not sulking when I have been an errant and difficult child
when I slip my hand into his
    and say forgive
  he squeezes my hand and smiles
    it's what he wanted all along
  the day
    although not perfect
      is not spoiled or wasted in his eyes

There will never be a perfect day. I know this...but still the tiny grains of disappointment and disillusionment can steal the true heart from each day. I can fall into the habit of missing the divine gifts because they are encased in soiled wrappings...the diamonds buried in midnight earth, the pearls in ugly clam shells, trusting smiles that light a dirty face, small hands that reach out after the tantrum has been spent. God, help me to seize the gifts of the day and cherish the divine things that grow from the dust of the earth.

FIRST HOME

Psalm 84:3-4 "Even the sparrow finds a home, and the swallow builds her nest and raises her young at a place near your altar, O Lord of Heaven's Armies, my King and my God! What joy for those who can live in your house, always singing your praises."

If asked what the perfect house would be, I would say Victorian, with balconies, stained glass, gingerbread trim, and bay windows...the bigger the better. This is my dream house.

When my husband and I began the search to buy our first home, my heart's prayer was, "Please God, a Victorian house with all the trimmings!" We looked at several homes, including large, lovely houses that whispered my name and stole my heart. In such a house, as I wandered through enormous rooms beguiled by my dreams, God spoke his thoughts into my heart: "This is more than you can handle now. You have two small children and a busy life. This house would consume you financially, physically and emotionally. You must trust me to give you what you need."

These were not the words I wanted to hear. Couldn't God do the impossible? Couldn't he open the doors and make a way for me? Haven't I waited long enough? But in the end, I laid my dreams on the altar, and God gave us a little, blue ranch house in the country with 900 sq. feet of living space and a yard full of pine trees. It was here that we raised our boys; here we made our memories. It was the home that I needed, the house that did not consume me, but gave me the ability to stay home and raise my family.

And there were moments of overwhelming beauty in this house...the afternoon sun filtering through ferns that twined together like school girls holding hands in the window...the graceful curve of dark, antique wood against pale green walls...the scent of pine coming in on breezes and lifting lace curtains like veils from the faces of the windows. I planted huge flower gardens along the outer edges and found the beauty that my heart hungered for, and it was enough.

While it is hard to let go of dreams, it is essential to realize that not every prayer will be "Yes." God knows far better than I do what I need and what I can handle. He also knows my heart and the things that stir the artistic nature that he gave me. He knows my thirst for beauty and even though he had to tell me "No"...I believe he understood why I had to ask. God balances and tempers my life. He continues to remind me as I lay my requests before him: "I know what you can handle. You're going to have to trust me to give you what you need...not always what you desire."

God kept my request tucked away in his pocket, and many years later at the right time and the right season of life, God gave me my Victorian home. And it was a house filled with fireplaces and stained glass, carved woodwork and bay windows. It was everything that I ever dreamed of, and so much more. I am humbled by the fact that God never forgot the immature and untimely request of his little girl, and in his heart he kept it...even after I forgot, he kept it. When the time was right, he pulled the gift from behind his back and said, "I have a surprise for you!" It was in his heart to give it all the time.

JUST LIKE DAD

DAD

I Corinthians 4:15 "For even if you had ten thousand others to teach you about Christ, you have only one spiritual father. For I became your father in Christ Jesus when I preached the good news to you."

I Corinthians 11:1 "And you should imitate me, just as I imitate Christ."

Psalms 37:23 "The Lord directs the steps of the godly. He delights in every detail of their lives."

Psalm 103:13 "The Lord is like a father to his children, tender and compassionate to those who fear him."

In your footsteps I will follow
I want to walk just like you do
no one else is like my Daddy
and no one else can fill your shoe

as our feet walk on together
you go ahead I come behind
teach my feet to follow Jesus
you take God's hand then hold mine

today Dad my feet are tiny
tomorrow they will be full grown
so today your hand must guide me
tomorrow's walk will be my own

It all started with a birthday gift for my husband, a plaster cast of the footprint of our not yet one-year old son. Such a tiny, little foot, "Where are you going?" I thought, and "What will your life be like?" As I held the imprint of that foot in my hand I saw my son following after my husband, carefully placing his little feet into the footprints that went ahead of him. I knew he had a good path to follow.

It is an awesome privilege and responsibility to be a father. No one else can inspire and give identity and direction to a child in the powerful way that a father can. From their first steps, my boys constantly followed after their Dad, reaching to hold his hand, wanting to be exactly where he was and to do exactly as he did. As the years went by, the expression of that need changed, but the reality of the need for a father never changed. Instead of holding his hand, they asked for his advice; instead of imitating him, they looked for his approval, praise and validation; instead of placing their tiny feet in the big prints that went ahead of them, they begin to walk beside him...their own footprints growing larger with each passing year.

Now, the walk is their own. They have forged a new path, but they stay true to the direction they learned so long ago, when they followed after their Dad.

SEEDLINGS

SEEDLINGS

Proverbs 21:2 "People may be right in their own eye, but the Lord examines their heart."

Proverbs 19:2 "Enthusiasm without knowledge is no good; haste makes mistakes."

Proverbs 3:11-12 "My child, don't reject the Lord's discipline, and don't be upset when he corrects you. For the Lord corrects those he loves, just as a father corrects a child in whom he delights."

Yesterday I tried to transplant downy-soft African Violet seedlings from their nursery pots into larger pots...and my son helped. And as I carefully blended and measured my soil and filled the pots, my son poured soil from pot to pot to shirt to table to floor, and we had to stop and clean it up.

And as I carefully lifted each fragile plant from old pot to new; separating, protecting and gently pressing each one into newer and richer soil, my son grabbed a plant and, before I could intervene, he smushed it down hard into a waiting pot, gave it a few good whacks and looked for another. As I pulled the mangled, broken plant from his hand, he cried from the insult of it all. Couldn't he plant just as well as I? And my patience slowly began to unravel.

I thought of you, Lord.

Why doesn't your patience unravel too, when so many of your little children try so hard to help? Think of all the spilled soil so carelessly wasted by self-satisfied children with no ear to hear instruction.

As I'm throwing away seedlings mangled and broken by overzealous hands, I wonder how many mangled things you have held, "smushed" by overconfident children that wanted to help in their own way and not yours? My seedlings are beyond repair, but I know in your hand all can be restored and redeemed.

I wonder, God, do you grieve for the needless things broken, the words spoken without knowledge, and judgments given without wisdom? And the errant child held screaming in indignation on your lap, do you still love?

I know you do. How many times have I been held there myself, and when the tantrum is spent, there is the loving breast to lean upon and the gentle lessons of discipline to be learned. You direct my steps with patience and you do not allow me to go my own way without correction. It is my choice to learn and obey.

Jesus,
   give me an ear to hear
   an eye to see
   a heart to obey
 your way, O Lord,
    your way
   and not my own.

VALENTINE'S DAY

Luke 10:27 "...You must love the Lord your God with all your heart, all your soul, all your strength and all your mind..."

Proverbs 23:26 "O My son, give me your heart. May your eyes take delight in following my ways."

Lamentations 3:41 "Let us lift our hearts and hands to God in heaven..."

> A heart for my teacher
> and one for my friend
> a heart for the preacher
> and many to send
> a heart for my mother
> and one for my dad
> a heart for my brother
> or else he'll be mad
> hearts that tell you how much you're adored
> but tell me who has a heart for the Lord

On a day when hearts are flying off in all directions and to every imaginable friend, family member, and acquaintance...there is a still, small voice that whispers, "My child, give me your heart."

He wants my heart, not a red paper cutout glued with lace and scrawled with crayoned words of love and devotion, but a living heart fixed on him and devoted to him.

Many years ago I read a poem by an unknown author.

> "I gave my father a valentine
> It had his name in a heart with mine
> It had my name in a heart with his
> And three silver cupids blowing a kiss
> He was surprised at the cupid part
> But he said he was used to my name in his heart."

God is used to my name in his heart. He thinks about me, even when I am not thinking about him. He has plans for me, he watches over me, he directs my steps, he will never leave me or forsake me...he is with me.

But do I have a heart for the Lord? Like a paper valentine, my heart can be blown about by the winds of life. It slides under the clutter and hides in the brightly colored ribbons twining my day. I mean to bring my heart to him...I mean to talk to him and stay in a place where I can see him, but other things crowd in front of me and I am overwhelmed and distracted.

But today, God, today I want to write your name in my heart. Today I want to bring you my valentine; I want to lift up my heart and hands to my God in heaven. Today I will have a heart for the Lord.

A FALL PICNIC

Psalms 145:15-16 "The eyes of all look to you in hope, you give them their food as they need it. When you open your hand, you satisfy the hunger and thirst of every living thing."

Ecclesiastes 3:1 "For everything there is a season, a time for every activity under heaven."

I took my boys on a fall picnic. Leaves blew everywhere in layers of gold and orange and crunched like corn flakes under our feet. We ran in the leaves, raked up great piles to jump in, tossed leaves high in the air to rain down again on our heads; it was a time to play and we did it whole-heartedly.

When it was time for lunch, I spread out a soft flannel blanket laden with hearty sandwiches, fruits, cookies...all the things my boys loved to eat. I called my sons, but they didn't want to stop the games they were playing...

Breathless, they chased leaves, flying farther and farther away from the boundaries that kept them safe. Every time I called them back, they came reluctantly, but soon they were again chasing the paper-thin bits of red and gold, and the afternoon flew away like the leaves. I knew my children were hungry, but the temptation to continue to play was too great. They circled close to me, grabbed a cookie, a handful of chips or a piece of fruit, and then ran away again full of giggles and shouts.

Finally I gathered up the picnic, mostly uneaten, and prepared for the long ride home. Secured within the boring confines of the car, it didn't take too long for the complaints to start.

"I'm hungry. Can't we stop and eat now?"

I saw their little faces in the rearview mirror, and I had to tell them, "No. It's late and we have to go home. Why didn't you eat when the food was waiting for you?"

But I already know the answer. They couldn't deny themselves the joy of one more run through the leaves...not for something as ordinary as a sandwich and a piece of fruit. Soon I can give them a proper meal. Soon we will be home. But I think of another picture and another meal.

God has spread his own picnic before me. On the blanket there is everything that I need for strength and nourishment to sustain me in the days to come. He is careful to make sure that the provision comes at just the right time. He sees what is to come. But sometimes I don't want to sit still. I'm busy. It's not convenient. I'm not hungry right now. But later, from the confines of events and emotions that I did not see coming, I cry out to him…"God, feed me now! Help me now!"

He does help me, but there is also the gentle reminder. "All day you ran away from me chasing your own golden leaves. Tell me, the leaves that you gathered while I waited, what are they like now?"

I have to admit they are dried and faded. I exchanged the pleasures of the moment for the time I could have spent with him. It was his peace I needed, his words, his comfort…not my dried and crumbling fancies.

Tʜᴇ Gᴏᴏᴅ Oʟᴅ Dᴀʏs

Ecclesiastes 7:10 "Don't long for 'the good old days.' This is not wise."

Ecclesiastes 5:19 -20 "...to enjoy your work and accept your lot in life - this is indeed a gift from God. God keeps such people so busy enjoying life that they have no time to brood over the past."

Ecclesiastes 6:9 "Enjoy what you have rather than desiring what you don't have. Just dreaming about nice things is meaningless - like chasing the wind."

Philippians 4:11-13 "...I have learned how to be content with whatever I have. I know how to live on almost nothing or with everything. I have learned the secret of living in every situation, whether it is with a full stomach or empty, with plenty or little. For I can do everything through Christ, who gives me strength."

I Timothy 6:6 "Yet true godliness with contentment is itself great wealth."

Cleaning the closet was long overdue, and from the hidden depths I extracted dress after dress from my past...flowing, bohemian dresses from my 70's college days, dresses for special occasions wrapped in protective plastic, even a few "curtain dresses" from the struggling years when I was first married. With no money for clothes, I had sewn dresses from some voluminous curtains that once hung in my windows. The right thing to do was to place all these dresses in the donate or throw-away pile...but I had difficulty doing it. I would take them up, and then lay them back down on the bed to consider one more time. Maybe I would wear them again...maybe I could reuse the material...maybe...

In a moment of revelation, God showed me the real reason for my hesitation. The dresses on the bed were the physical evidences of the woman I used to be. There was the college woman with the long flowing hair and a whole life yet to live, the woman attending her wedding shower, her baby shower, an anniversary dinner, a young mother struggling to make ends meet...keeping the dresses was like keeping a doorway open to the past. In subtle ways, the dresses whispered a longing to be again the woman that I once was. But the finality of God's word pierced my heart: "You will never again be that woman. You must lay it behind you and move on. Who you are now, by grace and growth, is far different and you cannot clothe that person with the past. Let go...don't long for what once was, it only steals the joy from what is."

I looked at my dresses and remembered past joys and sorrows, poignant and mellowed by years. The memories crowded together with colors and textures that

I wanted to hold and feel again…perhaps if I just slipped on a dress? The present is not as appealing, often full of hard work, tedious routine, worries, and difficulties that the past forgets. Today is not like the days when I wore those dresses. But today is all I have. I cannot go back, and the desire to do so is defeating…a thief biting into the fabric of the present. I let go.

Contentment operates in the present, the ribbon tying up the life that I now live. To find true contentment I cannot long for the "good old days." I cherish my memories, but I cannot long to relive them. My grasp is on the present and here I must rest my heart.

MOM'S MIXING BOWLS

TASTE AND SEE

Psalm 34:8 "Taste and see that the Lord is good. Oh, the joys of those who take refuge in him!"

I Peter 2:3 "now that you have had a taste of the Lord's kindness."

Psalm 119:103 "How sweet your words taste to me; they are sweeter than honey,"

1 Corinthians 2:9 "...No eye has seen, no ear has heard, and no mind has imagined what God has prepared for those who love him."

When I was a child there were wonderful moments in my mother's kitchen when she would whip up a cake or a batch of cookies in a large, yellow mixing bowl. When the last of the cake batter was poured into the pan, or the last cookie was placed on the sheet to bake, then there would be the glorious task of licking the bowl. There were often quite copious amounts of batter clinging to the sides; it had to be shared three ways between my brother, my sister and me. When her appreciative helpers were done, it almost seemed redundant to wash the bowl; it was already licked spotlessly clean.

When I became a mother and experienced the watchful eyes of my own children fixed upon my yellow mixing bowl, I always thought of my mother. I remember the day when I first realized the kindness expressed in that mixing bowl. I was making a cake and with my spatula, I had swiped the mixing bowl perfectly clean. I remembered thinking, "I wonder why my Mom could never get her bowls clean? She always used a spatula. Where had she gone wrong?" As soon as the words took shape in my mind, the truth gripped my heart. She always made us feel like important helpers who were cleaning up the mess she left behind...a very, very tasty mess. But the truth was, she did it all for us. I sat down at the table and let the revelation sink in. How I missed my Mom. How I wished I could say the thank you that came to my heart now.

For the first time I saw life from the other side of the mixing bowl. Of course my Mom could scrape a bowl clean with a spatula, but her heart was focused on us, not her talents and abilities. She wanted us to have the anticipated pleasure of tasting and knowing what goodness she was preparing for us. She didn't just leave a little bit, she left enough for three scrambling children get a good, solid taste of all the pleasures yet to come.

And so God says to me, "taste and see that I am good." He always leaves me a sampling on the sides of the day of the joys and glories he is preparing for those who love him. He includes me in his work, letting me sit beside him while he creates beautiful things yet to be. He doesn't hurry me away, but he makes time for me and listens to my questions. He shares his work with me, and always I am allowed to sample the goodness that will come when his work is completed. There is such sweetness and joy and kindness in that simple act...the invitation to taste and see that he is good. It may not be time yet for the completed recipe still being perfected in the oven, but he leaves me generous samples in his bowl. My appetite is whetted, and I anxiously look forward to all that is still to come.

"Taste and see that the Lord is good. Oh, the joys of those who take refuge in him!"

LEAVING HOME

Ecclesiastes 3:1-4 and 11 "For everything there is a season, a time for every activity under heaven. A time to be born and a time to die. A time to plant and a time to har- vest. A time to kill and a time to heal. A time to tear down and a time to build up. A time to cry and a time to laugh. A time to grieve and a time to dance... Yet God has made everything beautiful for its own time. He has planted eternity in the human heart, but even so, people cannot see the whole scope of God's work from beginning to end."

Psalm 84:5-7 "What joy for those whose strength comes form the Lord, who have set their minds on a pilgrimage to Jerusalem. When they walk through the Valley of Weeping, it will become a place of refreshing springs. The autumn rains will clothe it with blessings. They will continue to grow stronger, and each of them will appear before God in Jerusalem."

Hot green tea spiced with jasmine
waits in a travel mug
as heads bend low
in prayer
at the kitchen table
It is time to send
from the steamy warmth of home
and the closeness of hands
the one who must journey away
at this hour of the morning
and in this normal
after breakfast way
he must go
and it will be different from now on

There comes a time for all parents when a child leaves home. There is a finality in the leaving and a knowledge that from this moment on, things will never be the same.

The leaving is bittersweet, but God has set pilgrimage in the heart of every child. He calls them to journey to their own Jerusalem, their own holy city of God. Inevitably there will be valleys of weeping along the way, and God must be the father who is there when we are not. The strength that comes only from the Lord must be tested, sometimes by fire. It is a journey of faith and temptation, of joy and sorrow, of triumph and failure, of hope and despair…and as a parent, I can call encouragement from the sidelines, and pray, always pray. But I cannot take this journey for my children. And if I do not let my children go, they cannot ascend from strength to strength until they appear before God at their own journey's end. I can not see the whole scope of God's work, and there are many unknowns and dangers along the way, but all things have a time and a season and God has made everything beautiful and right for its own time. So, I cheer and encourage and pray…but I let each child learn to walk alone with their God.

AZURE MOUNTAIN

Joshua 1:9 "This is my command - be strong and courageous! Do not be afraid or discouraged. For the Lord your God is with you wherever you go."

Psalm 31:24 "So be strong and courageous, all you who put your hope in the Lord!"

Gone to the Blue Mountain
  be back soon
his note is jumbled
  on the kitchen table
    with gum wrappers
      black wristwatch
   and extra keys
my son
  has emptied his pockets
    to climb unhindered
scattering behind
  little seeds
    to call him home again
he goes alone
  to the Blue Mountain
and I must open my hands
  to the paths that take him
but put away
  near my heart
  the seed of promise
  be back soon

When my boys were teenagers we vacationed one summer in Maine. One day we hiked along the great rocky cliffs plunging down to the ocean, wild, rugged and dangerous. As we climbed, we came to a fork in the path...one branch led to a much longer and more challenging walk along the cliffs, and one branch led back to the safety of a small town. I asked for the easy road back, but my son's eyes were on the cliffs, adventure, and challenge...he begged to be allowed to go on by himself. He was so sure he could do it, filled with the need to prove he had what it takes. But I was filled with a mother's fear...my eyes could only see the little boy, not the emerging man. That day I robbed my son of his opportunity to be strong and courageous.

I have long since repented to my son and to God for my behavior on that day. How easily I succumbed to fear and the lie that it was my job to keep everyone safe. In the years since, I have learned to let my sons climb their mountains. I want them to know what it is to be strong and courageous, because that is what God has called them to be.

How can anyone know their strength and courage unless it is tested? Boys must do this to become men...and mothers must let them go. In God's hands, the little boys will "be back soon." But, unless I let them go, they cannot come back as men.

MY CHRISTMAS TREE

CHRISTMAS IN MY HOME

John 3:16 *"For God loved the world so much that he gave his one and only Son, so that everyone who believes in him will not perish but have eternal life."*

John 14:27 *"I am leaving you with a gift - peace of mind and heart. And the peace I give is a gift the world cannot give. So don't be troubled or afraid."*

The Christmas tree is gold and green
and hidden treasures yet unseen
lie wrapped beneath its bough

The angel in the top most limb
seems poised to sing a holy hymn
but all is still for now

My hands are empty by my side
my work is done I'm satisfied
let Christmas Day begin

My hands are empty when I sense
the gentleness of God's presence
where is my gift for him

My hands are empty but I raise
them up to him in humble praise
and with my gift he smiled

The Christmas tree is green and gold
my father reaches down to hold
the hands of his own child

In endless preparations, God brings us back and says, "Remember me." One of my earliest Christmas memories is getting up before everyone else on Christmas morning and sitting in front of the Christmas tree singing every Christmas carol that I knew.

I was only a child, but I have the memory of feeling God with me in the hush of the morning, when no one else was stirring. The moment was for us alone.

Years since, whenever I search for the perfect Christmas memory, God always brings me back to this...a little girl in pigtails sitting at her Father's knee and singing the songs of Christmas. My heart is filled again with the longing for that intimacy...tidings of comfort and joy...silent and holy night.

God brings me back to this and whispers, "Remember me."

COULD MARY SEE?

Luke 2:4-7 "And because Joseph was a descendant of King David, he had to go to Bethlehem in Judea, David's ancient home. He traveled there from the village of Nazareth in Galilee. He took with him Mary, to whom he was engaged, who was now expecting a child. And while they were there, the time came for her baby to be born. She gave birth to her firstborn son. She wrapped him snugly in strips of cloth and laid him in a manger, because there was no lodging available for them."

Luke 2:19 "but Mary kept all these things in her heart and thought about them often."

a boy was born
on a cold morn
and laid on Mary's arm
did she kiss his brow
and promise how
she'd keep him safe from harm

Could Mary see
as she bent her knee
inside that humble shed
the pale moon's glow
through a barred window
cast a shadow on his bed

Of a cruel cross
sorrow and loss
the scars that he would bare
or were her eyes
on the star-filled skies
and the curling of his hair

In the joy of birth, there is the shadow of sorrow and death. When I first held my newborn son, I remember thinking, "O God, let him never go to war, keep him safe, let nothing ever break his heart…" - a mother's fierce desire to fight the shadows, to ask for impossible things.

In the pale light of the stable, what shadows touched Mary's heart and what did she think about as she held the baby who would become her own salvation? In the moment when her fierce love would gladly die for the child on her lap, did she know that one day that child would die for her?

Sometimes joy is birthed in pain and the knowledge of death adds precious value to life. Mary kept many things in her heart that day, but I would like to think that her eyes were on the star-filled skies, and the curling of his hair. I believe with great joy she celebrated the birth of her son, and her Savior...just as we celebrate that birth today.

TO SEE THE FACE OF GOD

Matthew 2:1-2 and 9-11 "Jesus was born in Bethlehem in Judea, during the reign of King Herod. About that time some wise men from eastern lands arrived in Jerusalem, asking, 'Where is the newborn king of the Jews? We saw his star as it rose, and we have come to worship him.' ... And the star they had seen in the east guided them to Bethlehem. It went ahead of them and stopped over the place where the child was. When they saw the star they were filled with joy! They entered the house and saw the child with his mother, Mary, and they bowed down and worshiped him. Then they opened their treasure chests and gave him gifts of gold, frankincense, and myrrh."

Who can see a King
in shepherd form
manger born
and call him Lord

Who sees a Savior
crucified
and denied
and still believes

Who can see God
with earthly eyes
when some disguise
might hide his grace

He who has eyes to see
and ears to hear
when he appears
shall see his face

At the end of their long, arduous journey, the wise men saw the face of God. A humble room, common parents, no visible wealth or greatness, but they had eyes that saw beyond, ears that heard more, and hearts that believed greater. The disguise of ordinary was stripped away and they entered the throne room of God through a stark and rough hewn door.

In an instant, everything can change. Though the journey may seem common, ordinary, and tedious, there will be many rough hewn doors through which I will step, to suddenly behold the face of God.

THE TREE OF LIFE

Proverbs 11:30 "The seeds of good deeds become a tree of life..."

Proverbs 13:12 "Hope deferred makes the heart sick, but a dream fulfilled is a tree of life."

Psalm 104:16-17 "The trees of the Lord are well cared for - the cedars of Lebanon that he planted. There the birds make their nests, and the storks make their homes..."

Isaiah 61:3 "To all who mourn in Israel, he will give a crown of beauty for ashes, a joyous blessing instead of mourning, festive praise instead of despair. In their righteousness, they will be like great oaks that the Lord has planted for his ownglory."

```
        Christmas Eve
           walking my dogs through drifting
               gentle falling snow
        I saw a tree
            blue spruce
          tall as a good sized house
               and wide
             full and fat with health and tree-ish strength.
        and it sang to me
             the song of a myriad sparrows
                 tucked up inside its branches
             winking in and out of the shadowed depths
                 like tiny Christmas lights
        it made me stop
             and pulled me from my reverie of dog-walking thoughts
                 to gaze in wonder
          no other soul on the streets
               no other sound but the song of birds
                 then I heard God whisper
          what do you think of my Christmas tree
```

As proud as I was of my own Christmas tree, heavy-laden with antique and handmade ornaments, I had to admit that I had never seen a Christmas tree as spectacular as that blue spruce alive with singing birds. "You win, God! There has never been a tree like this!"

This tree, God's Christmas tree, was a tree full of life…vibrant and bursting with its own health, but carrying within its branches the ornaments of beauty and joyous, living praise. On this frosty night, in this miraculous moment, God shared his tree with me and I found hope and strength for the journey ahead. There had been a season of mourning and ashes, a season not entirely over yet, but in this moment God reminded me that he is the one who gives beauty for ashes and joy for mourning. It is in his heart to make me like this tree, a tree bursting with life and filled with the melodies of praise…a planting of the Lord, made for his glory.

FORGET ME NOT

FORGET-ME-NOT

Matthew 6:30 "And if God cares so wonderfully for wildflowers that are here today and thrown into the fire tomorrow, he will certainly care for you. Why do you have so little faith?"

Matthew 6:32-33 "...your heavenly Father already knows all your needs. Seek the Kingdom of God above all else, and live righteously, and he will give you everything you need."

Isaiah 49:15 "...Can a mother forget her nursing child? Can she feel no love for the child she has borne? But even if that were possible, I would not forget you!"

One morning, walking my dogs, I passed by a flower garden resplendent in sky-blue forget-me-nots. I breathed a quick sigh of a prayer... "O God, I wish I had forget-me-nots in my garden." And then I walked by.

The day was sunny and I walked slowly, enjoying the time away from schedules and responsibilities. The flower garden soon faded from thought as my mind wandered to other things. Then, I caught a glimpse of something that seemed out of place on the edge of the road. As I approached, I could see it was a plant. As I got closer, I saw it was a flowering plant, and when I finally reached it, a perfect bunch of sky-blue forget-me-nots nodded placidly in the breeze. The leaves were not wilted and although it had been removed from the ground, the roots were intact; it was a perfect plant, sitting patiently at the side of the road.

I heard the words, "For your garden."

My prayer, my oh-so-slight, sigh of a prayer had not escaped my Father's ear. He heard me. It was just a little bunch of wildflowers, but God paid attention to me. And if he cares so wonderfully for the wildflowers, if he cares so wonderfully for me, how can I doubt that he knows all my needs and he will take care of me in all things.

I will never forget the day my Father gave me a bouquet of flowers. It was a moment when he said, "I see you." He met me when I did not expect him to even be thinking about me, and he gave me flowers.

It has been many years since I picked up that bunch of forget-me-nots and walked home to plant them in my garden. They have grown and spread so that now the gardens on every side of my house are full of forget-me-nots. They surround me, and all that is in my house and all that is mine. They may disappear from sight for a winter season, but that does not mean God has forgotten me.

When the season is past, the flowers bloom again in even greater quantities. Everywhere I look there are patches of sky-blueness and I hear the words repeated, "I see you. I know your name. I will not forget you."

WATER LILY

GIFTS FROM CHILDREN

Isaiah 66:1 "... Heaven is my throne, and the earth is my footstool. Could you build me a temple as good as that? Could you build me such a resting place? My hands have made both heaven and earth; they and everything in them are mine. I, the Lord, have spoken! ..."

Psalm 116:12-13 "What can I offer the Lord for all he has done for me? I will lift up the cup of salvation and praise the Lord's name for saving me."

Psalm 63:4 "I will praise you as long as I live, lifting up my hands to you in prayer."

My son
  does not buy flowers in a store
    tissue paper swaddled
      with tags and pedigrees
  he brings me
    a single
      slightly opened
    water lily bud
        yellow
  still dripping lake water
    which has buoyed it up
      to catch the sunlight
        tempting his hand
          as he glides by with silent oar
  wild, fresh
    reminding me of rain and
      wind dipped in pine
  I rest it on silver-weathered planks
    lest I crush
  the fragile beauty
    still breathing within

There is something about a gift from my son, spontaneous and unplanned, that reaches into my heart and touches depths that ordinary life cannot reach. It demonstrates the action of love struggling to express itself when words are not always easy. My son knows that I have a passion for flowers, and in the midst of his adventuring, he has stopped to share with me a bit of beauty that catches his eye...and in sharing it, his actions say, "I thought about what would give you joy...I thought about you...I love you."

Sometimes I try to give God a gift that he does not need. I want to build him a temple of self-sacrifice and good works. But he already has a temple more beautiful than I could make. He is looking for something simple: a moment of un-solicited spontaneity, when I lift my hands to him so we can share an experience together. That is the gift that reaches his heart. I can feel God place his hand on my head as we share that moment of love, and even laughter. What can I give to God for all he's done for me? I'll lift my hands up to him in joy and gratitude and share with him my heart.

WINDFALL POND

Ezekiel 34:25-26 "I will make a covenant of peace with my people and drive away the dangerous animals from the land. Then they will be able to camp safely in the wildest places and sleep in the woods without fear. I will bless my people and their homes around my holy hill. And in the proper season I will send the showers they need. There will be showers of blessing."

In the proper time, there will be showers of blessing. My requests often comes out of season. In the earnestness of the moment, inspired by longing and sometimes feelings of destiny, the cry comes out. Sometimes the cry is loud and emotional. Other times, in the presence of seeming impossibilities, the prayer is not even uttered, it is only a sigh. But the prayer rises up to the throne of God, and he hears, and he keeps it, and he never forgets what has been whispered in his ear. And sometimes, even the most impossible prayer, even the prayer long ago forgotten or abandoned, finds the right season...and God delights to bring the answer.

When my children were little and our finances were limited, I have the memory of such a prayer. We were visiting one of the great Adirondack camps on a clear summer day...a family outing with aunts and uncles visiting from afar. In one of the beautifully restored guest cottages, amid the rustic timbers and neatly piled woolen blankets on camp beds, I breathed the little prayer, "O God, I wish I could give my children a few nights in a cabin like this, on a lake just like this one." I have the snapshot memory of where I was standing, and how the light shone in the window warming the blankets on the beds as I sighed that silent request.

Years passed and my boys grew up and left home. The time for such a prayer to be answered had come and gone. But, there came a summer with chance encounters, that are not really chance or coincidence, and the long forgotten prayer was given an answer. An impossibility became a reality and my husband and I were staying in a beautiful cabin on a private estate with a private lake at our disposal...more beautiful even than the cabin of my memory. And our youngest son was with us, staying in his own private cabin on that same estate.

Every morning we woke to loons crying on the lake and deer grazing in an open meadow. There was a gazebo built out over the lake, perfect for morning coffee and contemplation...and even a chapel with great wooden chairs facing floor-to-ceiling windows over the lake. In the night, by firelight, we had long, deep-hearted conversations with our son as night breezes blew through the fingers of pines, scenting the air with their fragrance. God gave us those beautiful days of pulling together before we must travel apart. Within a few months our son would move across country and a new chapter of life would begin for us all. But, for those precious few days, it was just the three of us sharing our hearts and dreams together as the comfort of God covered us like a protective blanket.

Even now I feel so humbled by the gift. I remembered the long ago prayer. God brought me back to that moment and that totally impossible sigh of a young mother's heart and whispered in my ear, "I heard you."

Dancing With My Father

Zephaniah 3:17 "For the Lord your God is living among you. He is a mighty savior. He will take delight in you with gladness. With his love, he will calm all your fears. He will rejoice over you with joyful songs."

My Dad had been in the hospital for several days, but he had made steady progress and finally I received word that he could go home in the afternoon. I had spent the morning with my Dad; he watched TV and snoozed while I read a book. My Dad was not a man of many words, but we didn't need many words to enjoy our time together.

I remember very distinctly standing up and kissing my father and saying, "Dad, you're going home today!" I gave him a hug and said good-bye... I did not know that when I left the hospital my Dad would make the final journey to his eternal home. I had spoken the truth, my Dad went home that day. It was just not to the room that I had carefully prepared for him in my home. I am forever grateful that I was able to kiss him good-by, and tell him he would be going home. Those moments given from God are never coincidences... God gave me the comfort I needed for the journey ahead.

Several weeks before my Dad passed away I had a vivid dream of dancing with him. My father was an amazing dancer: tall, lean and full of grace and effort-less motion. It was always a thrill when he danced with me. He would twirl me off my feet and leave me pinked-cheeked, breathless and begging for just one more dance. In my dream my father was twirling me effortlessly through space and I remember the feeling that I had as a child being held in my Daddy's arms. I clung to the moment, while at the same time knowing it was a fleeting dream and I would wake up and it would be over.

I did wake up...but in the vivid aftermath of the dream, I felt God speak to me. "This is who your father really is...he is not the man you see confined to a wheelchair, his face, the unmovable mask left by Parkinson's disease. This is your father, laughing, dancing...full of life. This is who your father really is."

I know, now, that God was preparing me to let go...soon my Dad would be dancing again, released from the confines of age and disease. There was com-fort in knowing he would dance, and sorrow in knowing it would not be with me...

"But who will dance with me now, God? Who can dance like my Daddy?"

It took time before I was able to hear the answer, but the answer has always been with me. "I am the one who will dance with you."

It is God who takes my hand and pulls me out to the dance floor. He holds me close in his arms, where it is warm and safe and protected, and he twirls me through space...my feet barely touching the floor. He takes me slowly, so I can hear the whisper of his voice...and then sometimes faster so my heart pounds with excitement. He teaches me the steps, some dances more complicated than others...he gives me grace and poise and confidence to move through even the most intricate pattern and stamina for the fast polkas. It is God who rejoices over me with joyful songs; he delights in me with gladness, he celebrates with me in dance.

One day I will see my Daddy again in heaven, and dance with him as I did when I was a child. But until then, God holds out his hand to me and whispers, "May I have this dance?"

THE SARAH YEARS

Genesis 18:10-11 and 13-14 "... 'I will return to you about this time next year, and your wife Sarah, will have a son!' Sarah was listening to this conversation from the tent. Abraham and Sarah were both very old by this time, and Sarah was long past the age of having children... Then the Lord said to Abraham, 'Why did Sarah laugh? Why did she say, "Can an old woman like me have a baby?" Is anything too hard for the Lord? I will return about this time next year and Sarah will have a son.'"

Ezekiel 37:4-5 "Then he said to me, 'Speak a prophetic message to these bones and say, "Dry bones, listen to the word of the Lord!" This is what the Sovereign Lord says: "Look! I am going to put breath into you and make you live again."'"

The year I turned sixty I had a child. I was long past the years of child-rearing, content with the role of grandma, the quiet house, time alone with my husband, readily available solitude; I was happy.

But God gave me a child...not an infant, but a child just a little past her teen-age years. In my old age, God gave me a child full of energy and need, joy and sorrow, hurt and incredible ability to survive, recklessness and humor...a child who burst the solitude like a bright red balloon on a hot radiator. In my settled, ordered life, God gave me a child who skipped and ran and shouted and took the stairs three at a time, and broke things, and lost things...a child whose sheer energy confounded my arthritic joints and predictable routines. God gave me a child and said, "These are your Sarah years. You are not done yet. You raised boys, now raise my daughter."

My Sarah years... What if I had said, "No?"

I did not know then what I know now, that this was my child of joy. That in difficult times she would lighten my load, that her energy would fight the darkness, that her love would round out the empty places and fill up the holes. I didn't know that my boys would love her as a little sister and pull her into their lives and hearts. I didn't know she would make my husband laugh...the laugh we had forgotten, the joy that had drifted and become calmer and more mature...until she came.

I didn't know that she would make me young again. I didn't know that inside this old body there was still energetic youth waiting to find a pathway to the surface. I didn't know that I could be a Sarah...that dried bones could be made to live, that I could have a child in my old age.

"Can an old woman like me have a baby? Is anything too hard for the Lord?"

There is a future hidden in God's hands that I know nothing about. This is a world where God speaks to the dry bones and the visions and dreams of youth visit us again in a different age. When my boys were still just toddlers, I had a collection of tiny pink dresses tucked away in a drawer for the little girl that I knew someday that I would have. It never happened for me. The dresses were given away unused, and the hope died. I went on and forgot the dream.

But like a grain of wheat fallen into the ground and forgotten, after years of dormancy, life unexpectedly stirs. The plant flourishes and blooms, but not anything like I had envisioned or planned. It is altogether different, but still the same.

There are Sarah years yet to be lived and dry bones waiting to be spoken into life.

HOLD TIGHT

HOLD TIGHT

Isaiah 46:3-4 "... I have cared for you since you were born. Yes, I carried you before you were born. I will be your God throughout your lifetime - until your hair is white with age. I made you, and I will care for you. I will carry you along and save you."

Isaiah 46:9-10 "Remember the things I have done in the past. For I alone am God! I am God, and there is none like me. Only I can tell you the future before it even happens. Everything I plan will come to pass, for I do whatever I wish."

Proverbs 16:31 "Gray hair is a crown of glory; it is gained by living a godly life."

Let me be
in old age
someone who
runs laps
around the kitchen table
chasing down memories
one by one
to clink together
in my calico button bag
shiny colored moments
that held us together
as family
now is not the time to let go
hold tight
hold tight
the fabric is old and frayed
but the buttons
are still young and hard and strong
hold tight

Some days I sit with my photo albums and scrapbooks and hold tightly to the memories of the past. I am a saver... I collect the little trinkets of life and tuck them away in boxes to eventually be fixed securely to construction paper pages with sticky bits of tape. I am not a fancy scrapbooker. There are no floral or pattered pages with fancy script titles and sophisticated, store-bought doodads to decorate. It's all bare bones for me...just my bits and pieces of memories all jumbled together and, in a comforting way, that is enough. They speak to me just the way they are and in most cases, they were never fancy to begin with. They are the memories of my family...God's grace in hard times, good times celebrated, milestones reached, things gained, things lost, and the odd little notes of ordinary days that touch my heart the most. I look through the memories of my life and see the thread of God's goodness that binds them all together...a paper quilt that warms my heart.

I am the keeper of the family, and I hold tight to the precious little scraps that celebrate our love and our story...a story like no other, God's story revealed in us.

WAITING FOR US TO COME HOME

Exodus 19:4 "...You know how I carried you on eagles wings and brought you to myself."

Psalm 116:15 "The Lord cares deeply when his loved ones die."

God, are you waiting for us to come home
Does your heart yearn for us
   waiting for that day when we can be
    home with you

I wait for my children to come home
    in airports
   I wait for my boys to return from
    far away places
called home sometimes in sorrow
    at someone's passing
   called to come on wings
    fly home
   so we can be together
  gather in the kitchen
the yellow light mingled with pots and pans
    aromas of spice and fruit
   windows that let the light seep out into the darkness
    telling the world we are home
  we are at the table
    we have stories to tell
  and memories
    more vivid than snapshots
    and laughter
   even in sorrow
  because we are family
   and sorrow cannot erase
    the joy that has been
   and will be again

God, are you waiting for us to come home
Does your heart yearn for us
   waiting for the day when we can be
    home with you

I know the intensity of my longing when I am waiting for my children to come home. As the day approaches, the longing grows stronger and stronger. And so, I believe, God is waiting for us to come home. In a moment, he calls and we fly home to him. Absent here, from the arms of those we love, but present with the Father. We will be at his table, holding his hand, with stories to tell and memories more vivid than snapshots… Home at last.

GOD IN MY HEART

HELD IN MY HEART

God in my Heart

A more private place...the heart. Here at the very core of my being I am molded, shaped...changed. God draws back the veil and I catch a glimpse of his face, feel the touch of his hand, hear the whisper of his voice. He challenges me in the way I see myself, in the way I see him, in the way I handle situations and respond to people. God wants me to grow up in him, just as I want my own children to grow and mature...and so he deals with my heart, but always gently and with great compassion. He does not let me hide or refuse to see what he must show me. He teaches me to love his law and the word that changes me from the inside out.

Psalm 119:10-11

"I have tried hard to find you -

don't let me wander from your commands.

I have hidden your word in my heart,

that I might not sin against you."

Psalm 119:28-29

"I weep with sorrow;

encourage me by your word.

keep my from lying to myself;

give me the privilege of knowing your instructions."

A PLACE IN YOUR ARMS

Deuteronomy 33:27 "The eternal God is your refuge, and his everlasting arms are under you..."

Sometimes at night when my strength is all spent
overwhelmed with unending tasks
there's one last request I'm longing to make
but I don't feel worthy to ask

Lord, I really want a place in your arms
safe from relentless demands
I am not good at just being your child
and coming with such empty hands

Lord, I really want a place in your arms
I'm tired of playing this part
of trying to earn a piece of your love
what I want is all of your heart

> Sometimes at night when your strength is all spent
> I patiently wait by your side
> ready to hold you and carry the pain
> you are trying so hard to hide
>
> I'm longing to hold you close in my arms
> there's nothing more you can do
> I'll carry your burden, give you my rest
> my arms are a shelter for you
>
> I'm longing to hold you close in my arms
> grieved at what keeps us apart
> I want much more than a piece of your life
> what I want is all of your heart

It turns out we want the same thing. All the pretense, the striving to be good enough, the acting out of parts...none of it has satisfied my heart that yearns for the heart of God. I want a place in his arms. God is longing for the same thing, the relationship that cradles his child safe in his everlasting arms, not the works and the pretense and the striving...just his child in his arms. We both are longing for the heart.

§

Swing Out

LET FAITH SWING OUT

Luke 1:37 "For nothing is impossible with God."

Matthew 19:26 "Jesus looked at them intently and said, 'Humanly speaking, it is impossible. But with God everything is possible.'"

Hebrews 11:1 "Faith shows the reality of what we hope for; it is the evidence of things we can not see."

2 Corinthians 5:7 "For we live by believing and not by seeing."

On a swing
    thrusting my toes up into heaven
    I pretend to walk on the green leaves
        brushed with each arc of flight
    into the treetops I ascend
        walking on the sky
    a place I have no business being
        an impossible place
        but I swing out
        and make it mine
let faith swing out
        in such a way
    and set my toes on heaven's shores
a place where I have no business being
        if it were just me
        on my own
    but I have grabbed the seat of faith
        and knotted my hands in hope
    and so swing out
through clear blue sky
        brushing my toes on impossible things
        as if I could stand among them
        by his grace
    and so perhaps I can

There is nothing quite so exhilarating as a swing. As a child, it was the closest that I came to flying. It took me off the ground and gave me the sky, and the lush green leaves. It set my face looking above, until I forgot the limits of earth and possible and common and ordinary. I let go of my earth-bound self and tried to become part of the sky...not so impossible as it had seemed only minutes before.

When I grab the seat of faith and swing out to God, there is a change in my perspective. Earth fades and I am closer to heaven than I was only minutes before. I brush my toes on the impossible, and it feels as if I might stand there... as if God will take my hand and pull me up beside him to see things as he does. The more I pump and push the swing, the more exhilarating the ride. Faith soars, there's a holy wind in my hair and warmth on my face. Earth fades and drops away with all its cares and worries until there is only sky and God and possible. Let faith swing out.

§

LOVE IS HARD

I John 4:20 "If someone says, 'I love God,' but hates a fellow believer, that person is a liar; for if we don't love people we can see, how can we love God, whom we cannot see?"

I John 4:16 "We know how much God loves us and we have put our trust in his love. God is love, and all who live in love live in God, and God lives in them."

I John 3:16 "We know what real love is because Jesus gave up his life for us. So we also ought to give up our lives for our brothers and sisters."

Hate is easy
revenge is easy
bitterness is easy
  it is the downhill journey
     the path of least resistance
  it requires so little of me
    a giving in
      a relinquishing of will
        a slight sigh of surrender
  all I have to think about is myself
    no one else to get in my way
love is hard
forgiveness is hard
sacrifice is hard
  it requires everything
    and is not an easy journey
  I must give up what I feel is my right
   for someone who may not deserve it
     in my eyes
if I do not love
will God live in me
   if I hate
     am I a liar playing at a game
       having no god
     but emotion

It is impossible to go too far in life without a face to face encounter with the reality of evil manifest in people and situations. In such times the easiest emotions are anger, resentment and bitterness. They flare to the surface with a desire for retaliation and can feed and nourish hatred. It is the easiest road, but not the best; ultimately it hurts me more than it could ever hurt anyone else. Love is hard, but it heals. Love delivers me from the responsibility of being judge and jury in situations where I only know part of the truth. Those tasks are given back to God, and I am free to move on.

§

A BROKEN AND REPENTANT HEART

Psalm 51:17 "The sacrifice you desire is a broken spirit. You will not reject a broken and repentant heart, O God."

Psalm 34:18 "The Lord is close to the brokenhearted; he rescues those whose spirits are crushed."

Joel 2:13 "'Don't tear your clothing in your grief, but tear your hearts instead.' Return to The Lord your God, for he is merciful and compassionate, slow to anger and filled with unfailing love..."

Whole I cannot use you
to hold my glorious light
but brokenness transforms
a vessel in my sight
paradox and puzzle
a mystery to man
broken vessels holds more
than whole ones ever can

Brokenness is a paradox....it should be my undoing, but it becomes my strength. It should destroy me, but it makes me a better person. It should disqualify me from service, but it enables me to serve in far greater ways. It should turn me in upon myself and make me introspective and self-absorbed, but it teaches me to give all the more to others.

In times of brokenness, there can be many questions. Sometimes there are answers that emerge on the journey and sometimes there are not. I have learned that things are best left in God's hands. I go through and I don't know why, but it changes me. I become a different person...hard places are worn down and made smooth and more gentle. I become more compassionate for the frailties and sufferings of others. My view changes, my patience stretches, my heart grows bigger as it is torn, and then mended and then torn again. But always my heart grows...always I grow. He is forming me to contain more of him than I ever thought possible...more of his light, more of his love...and all the broken places let the river of living water flow out to touch the hearts of others. He pours in, and out it flows, again and again and again.

WHEN I DON'T PRAY HARD ENOUGH

Proverbs 3:5 "Trust in the Lord with all your heart; do not depend on your own under-standing."

2 Corinthians 12:9 "... 'My grace is all you need. My power works best in weak-ness.'..."

When I don't pray hard enough
does God listen to me
when I am not good enough
O God what do you see

someone so unusable
so weak and anger prone
someone who can't do enough
to stand before your throne

if only I could be enough
to earn some of your grace
if I could just see enough
could I behold your face

there will never be enough
no deeds that I can do
I have to know my weakness
before I come to you

no beauty strength or effort
nothing my hands have made
substitutes for what Christ did
the ransom that he paid

I can never be enough
you became all for me
your grace more than sufficient
controls my destiny

I am a goal oriented person. It is my nature to want to make things better, more organized and more efficient. It is difficult for me to remember that God has not called me to fix life. When the things I pray for do not turn out as I anticipated, I can not manipulate the outcome by praying harder, working harder, or being more. It is not my diligence or strength that fixes anything, only God can do that. I bring my requests, but I must leave them in his hands. Prayer doesn't allow me to change life, it allows God to change me.

MY BLACKBOARD

THE BLACKBOARD

I Peter 5:7 "Give all your worries and cares to God, for he cares about you."

Matthew 6:34 "So don't worry about tomorrow, for tomorrow will bring its own worries. Today's trouble is enough for today."

Proverbs 12:25 "Worry weighs a person down; an encouraging word cheers a person up."

Lamentations 3:22-23 "The faithful love of the Lord never ends! His mercies never cease. Great is his faithfulness; his mercies begin afresh each morning."

Prayer erases worry.

In my schoolroom I have a blackboard. Every morning I write on the blackboard the problems for the day; math problems that my students will complete when they first come into the room and start to work. The problems may be varied; fraction problems, order of operations, word problems. They must be worked on, sometimes puzzled over, hopefully solved.

At the end of the day, I take my eraser and one by one I erase the problems from the board. Some of them were solved, some were not. Some of the problems frustrated, some annoyed, some puzzled, some were conquered...but at the end of the day I erase them all.

Although I erase all the problems, there is a residue of dust that remains. But, thankfully, during the night someone comes in and washes my board and in the morning it is once again pristine...waiting for new problems to be written upon it.

I can't help but see the similarity between my blackboard and my life. Every morning there are problems written upon my life...things that I must face during the day. All day I struggle through, but in the end, when I take it all to God in prayer, the problems are erased one by one. Some are solved...some are simply laid down at his feet because they are too hard for me, but I know he can handle them. So, I lay them down and run my eraser over them until they are reduced to dust. Then, when I walk away having left all in God's hands, the Holy Spirit comes in and washes away any dust and confusion still remaining. I wake up to a morning where God's mercies are new...my blackboard is wiped clean.

I know the new day will have its problems, but I am always heartened by the sight of my many erasers lined up on the blackboard tray. I know that when I choose, when I go to prayer...I take up an eraser and I wipe away a problem.

Imagine what my blackboard would look like if I never prayed, if I never wielded my eraser? What confusion...yesterday's problems blending into problems form a week ago and problems from a month ago. One half a train going to minus ten plus three at 45 mph in the opposite direction of two. Who could even begin to make sense of the confusion. Yet, when I do not pray, why am I surprised by the whirlwinds of fear and worry storming through my life? I have forgotten to erase; I have forgotten to lay the problems down at the foot of the altar and let go.

§

WORD OF THE DAY

Psalm 119:114 "...Your word is my source of hope."

Psalm 119:143 "As pressure and stress bear down on me, I find joy in your commands."

Psalm 119:28 "I weep with sorrow; encourage me by your word."

Psalm 119:37 "Turn my eyes from worthless things, and give me life through your word."

Hebrews 4:12 "For the word of God is alive and powerful. It is sharper than the sharpest two-edged sword, cutting between soul and spirit, between joint and marrow. It exposes our innermost thoughts and desires."

In my classroom I write a "Word of the Day" on the blackboard every morning. When my class comes in, we discuss the meaning of the word and practice using it correctly. My hope is that students will be able to add these words to their vocabulary, thus increasing their knowledge daily. No matter how inspired or relevant my word choices are, I recognize that vocabulary will not change a life. These are words, tools of language...but tools only.

There is, however, another word: a word that brings life and changes life.

I woke up one morning feeling a weight and unshakable darkness that made it difficult to perform even routine tasks. I could not clearly define where the feeling came from, but it covered everything and pulled me down into depths where I do not usually dwell.

It is my routine in the mornings to read my Bible. I read chronologically over the course of a year, starting at Genesis and reading through to Revelations. On this particular morning my reading began in one of the Old Testament books that contained chapter after chapter of genealogies...name after unpronounceable name. I do not remember the exact book, but I do know my thought was, "Great, this is really going to lift me out of my depression." And so, without much hope, I began to read.

But an unusual thing happened...as I began to read, the weight began to lift. As I stumbled through those lists of names, my heart began to calm... I felt peace seeping into my spirit and hope rising. It wasn't long before the darkness began to give way and I felt true and unexpected joy. In those moments, God gave me a revelation that I will never forget.

His word is living…all of his word…every name, every list, every detail, every fact, every Psalm, every gospel…all of God's word. At any moment and any time God can use any portion of his word to accomplish his purpose. It is alive and it moves and flows with the direction of the Holy Spirit. When in my weakness and insufficiency I do not know where to read or where to find help…God will give me what I need for the day if, in obedience, I seek him where he promises to be found. The very life of his word will do whatever God tells it to do. Every day he has a word for me, and that word brings spiritual nourishment and health.

There are many days when the truth of the living word is not so dramatically demonstrated in my daily reading…yet, in faith, I believe that every day life is being imparted as I invite his word to reside in me.

THE ALABASTER BOX

Mark 14:3-6 "...a woman came in with a beautiful alabaster jar of expensive perfume made from essence of nard. She broke open the jar and poured the perfume over his head. Some of those at the table were indignant. 'Why waste such expensive perfume?' they asked... But Jesus replied, 'Leave her alone. Why criticize her for doing such a good thing to me?'"

2 Corinthians 2:15 "Our lives are a Christ-like fragrance rising up to God..."

> I made an
>   alabaster box
> my treasures placed
>   within its locks
>
> The alabaster
>   cold as ice
> seemed such a worthy
>   sacrifice
>
> I gave the box
>   God looked within
> the handsome
>   alabaster skin
>
> and broke the shell
>   released the soul
> in brokenness
>   at last made whole
>
> the fragrance released
>   at his throne
> more precious than
>   the mask of stone

I try so hard to conceal my weakness and need, constructing strong, cold walls around everything that would betray me. I decorate those walls, hoping beauty might conceal the desperation within....and then I bring it to God. I hope he will not look too closely, because if he does he may throw away this box that contains all my secrets, all my hopes, all my fears. I've done my best to make the box beautiful and myself invisible. It is the only way I know.

But God is not fooled. He wastes little time with the box, knowing it must be broken. The treasure locked within is his goal: the soul he created, unbelievably costly and fragrant yet hidden and bound in darkness. "In brokenness I will release you," he whispers as he lets the box fall and shatter. And from the ruins he pulls me, in glorious fragrance, to dance before his throne.

DO YOU KNOW MY NAME?

Psalm 144:3-4 "O Lord, what are human beings that you should notice them, mere mortals that you should think about them? For they are like a breath of air; their days are like a passing shadow."

Psalm 139:17-18 "How precious are your thoughts about me, O God. They cannot be numbered! I can't even count them; they outnumber the grains of sand! And when I wake up, You are still with me."

Isaiah 43:1 "... 'Do not be afraid, for I have ransomed you. I have called you by name; you are mine.'"

John 10:3 "...He calls his own sheep by name..."

All I am is a puff of air
a shadow in the flame
God I wonder if you care
and do you know my name

What can I ever mean to you
and do you think of me
life is a vapor gone like dew
a bud cut from the tree

The grass withers the flower fades
I'm a wandering vine
from dust to dust my path is laid
in a circle of time

But your hand rests upon my hand
your thoughts encompass me
outnumbering the grains of sand
that rim the endless sea

No puff of air no shadowed thought
no ember without flame
I'm not forgotten not unsought
you've called me by my name

God, do you know my name? There is a longing to know, in the vast sea of humanity, God sees me....singular, insignificant, solitary...just me. And at the same time there is the fear....singular, solitary, insignificant...that I cannot be of importance in the mind of the Creator of all things. It is the cry of, "God do you know me?" and, at the same time, "God, how can you possibly know me?" And wondrously, in the midst of doubt, God comes and whispers my name. He knows me.

§

SEEING IN THE DARK

Matthew 4:16 "The people who sat in darkness have seen a great light. And for those who lived in the land where death casts its shadow, a light has shined."

Isaiah 9:2 "The people who walk in darkness will see a great light. For those who live in the land of deep darkness, a light will shine."

Daniel 2:22 "He reveals deep and mysterious things and knows what lies hidden in darkness, though he is surrounded by light."

I think that I see most clearly in the daylight. Everything is illuminated and made plain before me...there is no guessing about what is in my path or where I should set my feet as I walk through my day. I see it all clearly because it lies in the light.

But there is a paradox in this thinking. When do I see the farthest? The answer is this...only at night, in the darkness, as I gaze at the stars. I can see farther in the dark than in the day.

I would like my path to be always be in the light. I don't like the struggles of darkness. But in the bright light of day, this is the only world I can see. My vision turns inward and downward as I concentrate on living within the confines of what I see...my world, my planet, my sun which wakes me and warms me. Night calls my eyes up to the sky. I see beyond the brightness of my sun to behold a million more suns. Something expands within me as time and space grow before my eyes. I can believe for more because I can see more....limits drop away. Like a sigh escaping from a heart too long closed up, a weight escapes from a soul too long focused down on the solid ground beneath my feet. When I look at the stars, I begin to think of wings.

When the night seasons come in life, my eyes are forced to look up for help that will come from beyond the limits of what I can see and control. The darker the night, the brighter God shines. Without the night, I would never know the stars. Without the dark, I would never know the great light of God which shines out of the darkness. There are mysteries and things hidden in darkness that I can never know unless I travel into the darkness to see.

So often in the past my vocabulary of darkness has been a vocabulary of endurance, frustration, impatience, self-pitying, and long-suffering. I put life on hold while I tried to figure out what I did to get there and what I could do to get out as quickly as possible. But, seasons of darkness have been profound turning points in my life. It didn't matter how I got there, and I was never the one who had anything to do with getting out…in the darkness, I learned to open my eyes to see God. My words have turned to songs of praise to the Father who held me in sorrow, who took my hand in sickness and pain, who never left me alone in the dark.

God enables me to see farther in the dark than I can in the day.

§

TAKE MEASURE

THE MEASURING STICK

Ephesians 3:18-19 "And may you have the power to understand, as all God's people should, how wide, how long, how high, and how deep his love is. May you experience the love of Christ, though it is too great to understand fully. Then you will be made complete with all the fullness of life and power that comes from God."

Mark 4:24 "... The measure you give will be the measure you get back - and you will receive even more."

It is the measure of God's strength
   not my own
sometimes I use the wrong ruler
  I hold up my own small wooden stick
      twig-thin and pencil marked
   telling of weakness and lack
    and by it measure out my day
and when I see my inability
  I shrink in upon myself
   and try to hide in the undergrowth
    of excuses and apologies
tigers of fear
  roam about me
  gnawing on the edges of the day
   holding me penned
lulled almost to sleep
    in my hiding hole
then God
  who spans the universe with his fingertips
  begins to measure out my day
   not by my ability
    but by his

I hold up my fingertips to the heavens. My hand is so small in comparison to God's. But, he bends down to cover my hand with his own and gently whispers, "Let me do it..."

He has already measured out my day. He has gone behind me and before me and not one inch has escaped his notice. The measurement is perfect and precise, accurate beyond the abilities of man, and he tells me, "Everything lines up... This is the honest measurement of the day and truth lies only with me... You must trust me with this." I must trust him.

ℨ

LET YOUR WORDS BE FEW

Ecclesiastes 5:2 "Don't make rash promises, and don't be hasty in bringing matters before God. After all, God is in heaven, and you are here on earth. So let your words be few."

Isaiah 40:13-14 "Who is able to advise the Spirit of the Lord? Who knows enough to give him advice or teach him? Has the Lord ever needed anyone's advice? Does he need instruction about what is good? Did someone teach him what is right or show him the path of justice?"

Jeremiah 10:23-24 "I know, Lord, that our lives are not our own, we are not able to plan our own course. So, correct me, Lord, but please be gentle. Do not correct me in anger, for I would die."

Matthew 6:7-8 'When you pray, don't babble on and on as the Gentiles do. They think their prayers are answered merely by repeating their words again and again. Don't be like them, for your Father knows exactly what you need even before you ask him!"

In my immaturity and in the midst of my fears and my control issues inspired by those fears, I sometimes find myself telling God what he needs to do. God, in his mercy, meets me in my fears, but he also gently challenges my motives.

I often pray for situations that may arise during the course of the day. Sometimes, dramatic scenarios pop into my mind and I try to cover all the bases in my prayer. I ask God to do a myriad of specific things that sound good and reasonable at the time. There is a nervous energy that gets hold of me and I keep adding more detail, not wanting to leave anything uncovered or "left to chance." I am ordering and scripting my day and instructing God in his responses to my anticipated needs.

Very clear in my memory is the day God stopped me mid-prayer and spoke into my mind his thoughts on the subject. "I will do," He said, "the things that you ask me to do. But, I want you to understand that these things were not the things that I had in my mind to do. You ask for so much less than my best...you do not even know or comprehend my best. I would like you to ask me, 'God, give me what I need for the day.' and then trust me to do just that."

I stopped. A weight began to lift. "Yes, God, give me what I need for the day." What relief in those gentle words of correction. The burden to make the day successful is no longer my burden, hinging on the things I do or do not pray for. God knows what I need, and he is there to supply everything according to his riches.

I had been willing to settle for so much less.

I am not advocating less time in prayer, or the notion that each day all I need to say is, "give me what I need," and then be on my way. Every day there still must be intimate dialog with my Father and I am instructed by his word to "pray without ceasing."

But the prayers that are birthed out of my fear and my need to control; this is where God challenges me and I must learn to let my words be few. I tell him my needs and concerns, but his answers and the ways he choses to bring them about will be so much better than the very best I could imagine.

§

THE SECRET TRIAL

Isaiah 5:18 "What sorrow for those who drag their sins behind them with ropes made of lies, who drag wickedness behind them like a cart!"

Song of Solomon 2:15 "Catch all the foxes, those little foxes, before they ruin the vineyard of love, for the grapevines are blossoming!"

The secret trial
unspoken fear
nagging worry
unshed tear

these things become
a prison cell
chains bound tight with
never tell

circumvented
when I pray
I keep them hidden
let them stay

embarrassed that
I am so torn
by tiny pebbles
wobbly thorns

but hidden sins
are deadly seeds
unspoken hurts
unsaid needs

silent they grow
and take their ground
until I am
broken and bound

> by things too small
> to give to him
> defeated by
> a little sin

Is there something in my life that remains unspoken, some little thing that pales in comparison to larger trials and worries crowding it out? Is there something too small to mention to God? These are the very things that need to be spoken in confession and silenced in repentance. It can be the little things that spoil life and bring defeat.

STILL WITH ME

Psalm 139:18 "...and when I wake up, you are still with me!"

Psalm 139:1 and 5-6 "O Lord, you have examined my heart and know everything about me... You go before me and follow me. You place your hand of blessing on my head. Such knowledge is too wonderful for me, too great for me to understand!"

Are you still with me
  there are times when I
    do not want to be with me
     I am cranky, agitated
      sour
like a bitter cup of coffee
    roughly sloshed
      on books and dreams
       staining everything
 too much me
  too little you
     too much in my cup
   yet never full
  too much
   not enough
backward life
   that I live
  in hopes
    of going forward
why are you
  still with me
   no one else would stay
    like you do

I reach up for your hand. O God, you are still with me. I feel like such a hopeless case, but I want your hand. I can't even seem to pray, but I know that I need you. You know everything about me...no matter what I do, no matter what I say, no matter who I am...when I wake up, you are still with me. You know me. You see me when I sit down and when I stand up. You see me when I am at my worst…in that place I could never let anyone else go. You know everything I do. You know what I am going to say even before I say it. I ask the darkness to hide me, but to you the night shines as bright as day. Darkness and light are the same to you. Even there your hand guides me and your strength supports me. And every morning, every single morning…when I wake up, you are still with me. O God, there is no one like you!

§

The Center of the Circle

Luke 9:23 "... If any of you wants to be my follower, you must give up your own way, take up your cross daily, and follow me."

Revelation 7:17 "For the lamb on the center of the throne will be their Shepherd. He will lead them to springs of life-giving water. And God will wipe every tear from their eyes."

In the center of the circle
the lamb is on the throne
my thoughts and will are set aside
and he is Lord alone

In the center of the circle
I was surprised by pain
I thought within his perfect will
the world was mine to gain

In the center of the circle
instead I found a cross
someone to teach me sacrifice
a time to suffer loss

In the center of the circle
I found a threshing floor
where wheat was beaten from the chaff
and crushed to feed the poor

In the center of the circle
I found refiner's fire
melting from my impurities
the gold he did desire

It was mine to choose the center
or walk the outer rim
both paths would win me heaven's door
both paths led after him

The outside was the easy road
the smooth and well-worn part
but I chose to take the journey
through the center of his heart

Every choice we make has a cost. The deepest things go through to the center and cost everything...but in the end they will also give everything. The secret yearnings of our heart are only found in his heart, and he dwells in the center of all things. We must go deep to find him.

Nailed to the Cross

Colossians 2:13-15 "You were dead because of your sins and because your sinful nature was not yet cut away. Then God made you alive with Christ, for he forgave all our sins. He canceled the record of the charges against us and took it away by nailing it to the cross. In this way, he disarmed the spiritual rulers and authorities. He shamed them publicly by his victory over them on the cross."

I Peter 5:8-9 "... Watch out for your great enemy, the devil. He prowls around like a roaring lion, looking for someone to devour. Stand firm against him and be strong in your faith..."

He forgave all my trespasses
he took everything that
    shouted against me
      condemning me
and nailed it permanently to the cross
he spoiled the enemy
    ruined his power
      and triumphed over him openly
once and for all
    it was finished
but I live so often
  as if it were not so
condemned and defeated
  by only a shadow
not seeing that
    the roaring lion has no teeth
    and is fettered
      in chains of iron
    and I
am the one who is free

Satan would like to keep me bound in his kingdom of lies. He roams around me, inching closer, pulling in the circles of confinement with chains of deceit. He roars out his challenge and claims his power over me. It sounds so true, and as long as the blindfold of lies is pulled down over my eyes, I tremble in fear and retreat.

What if, instead, I allowed God to remove my blindfold? What if I called out to God for truth? Before me stands the enemy. The path that I thought hemmed me in, is in fact his path of confinement...the end of his tether. Thick chains bind him always to his distant path and keep me always out of harms way. When he roars...I see his jaws are toothless. I am the one who stands free. God has already won the victory, triumphing over the enemy openly. This is truth. This is what God has already done through the power of the cross.

§

BEYOND COMPREHENSION

Psalm 147:3-5 "He heals the brokenhearted and bandages their wounds. He counts the stars and calls them all by name. How great is our Lord! His power is absolute! His understanding is beyond comprehension!"

Psalm 8:1 and 3-4 "O Lord, our Lord, your majestic name fills the earth! Your glory is higher than the heavens... When I look at the night sky and see the work of your fingers - the moon and the stars you set in place - what are mere mortals that you should think about them, human beings that you should care for them?"

Psalm 139:6 "Such knowledge is too wonderful for me, too great for me to under-stand!"

Jeremiah 23:23-24 "Am I a God who is only close at hand?' says the Lord. 'No, I am far away at the same time. Can anyone hide from me in a secret place? Am I not everywhere in all the heavens and earth?' says the Lord."'

As if it were the most common thing
one hand upon my broken heart
binding a wound
about which
he knows every detail
bending down to listen
to my small voice
the other hand in the heavens
counting out the stars
by name
remembering the songs of creation
wrapping each one in God-light
to spin in his ethereal dance
he sees us all
and knows
beyond comprehension

One hand on Earth, the other hand in the heavens...and he knows. It stretch-es my mind. Do I go too far? But these are his words, his infallible, perfect words, and he has spoken these lines together as if there were the most natural connec-tion between them. He reaches down to brush my shoulder and he reaches up to grasp stars that have names and places in his memory.

Sometimes my mind needs to be stretched out. I have a tendency to relegate God to the limits of my own understanding, a place where he cannot possibly dwell.

I look up to the night sky. I let my gaze linger beyond the momentary glance that sees nothing. I consider the works of his fingers, the moon and the stars he has set in place and let the knowledge seep into me like the darkness seeps into the earth, cooling and refreshing. I am filled with awe and reverence. How absolute is God's power. HIs understanding is beyond comprehension; such knowledge is too wonderful for me, too great for me to understand.

§

SAFE IN THE LION'S MANE

LAMBS AMID THE LION'S MANE

Isaiah 40:11 "He will feed his flock like a shepherd. He will carry the lambs in his arms, holding them close to his heart. He will gently lead the mother sheep with their young."

Psalm 121:3 "He will not let you stumble; the one who watches over you will not slumber."

John 10:27-28 "My sheep listen to my voice; I know them, and they follow me. I give them eternal life, and they will never perish. No one can snatch them away from me."

Lambs amid the Lion's mane
sheltered by this robe
peering through the tangles
of tawny, twining gold

Lambs upon the Lion's breast
nodding drowsy heads
take their sleep in safety
upon their rumbling bed

Lambs between the Lion's paws
gambol out to play
kept between the hidden claws
that frighten harm away

Lambs drawn near the Lion's heart
hear the mighty beat
feel the breath of heaven
safe in their mercy seat

Safe...safe between the paws of the lion, safe to live life to the fullest...safe to play, safe to sleep, safe to lay my head upon his chest and look out at a world of uncertainty and feel no fear. God has me between his paws, he has me hidden within the tangles of his mane, he holds me close so I can hear his heart beat when I lay my head down in sleep, and even in dreams I know he is there. Though I am only a lamb, weak and often vulnerable, yet I am safe. I am with God, and he does not slumber or sleep.

§

FROM THE HEART OF THE FIRE

Deuteronomy 5:24 "...the Lord our God has shown us his glory and greatness, and we have heard his voice form the heart of the fire..."

Psalm 31:15 "My future is in your hands..."

My judgments expectations and decisions
    come from the outside edges
I look in as far as I can see
      but my vision is mortal
I see within the limits of time
      from a stationary point
          like the period at the end of a sentence
    I know that the story can change in an instant
      with the turning of a page in my book
but I see only my own sentence
      and myself positioned resolutely at its end
         all my future expectations rely on what has been written before
        and even then
          my memory is weak
but God calls from the heart of the fire
    no one else can go there
   no one else can speak from that place
      only God
I have wisdom from the outer edges
    and hear advice from others positioned on the outer edges with me
      who see as I do
         bound in time and fixed in space
but God
    who holds my times in his hands
      calls from the heart of the unknown
        from all that was and is and is to be
  I am before you and behind you
    I am the alpha and omega
   the beginning and the end
I hear his voice from the heart of the fire
    and I can rest in him

When I do not know, there is one who does. When I can not see, there is one who can. When I have come to an end, there is one who has no end or beginning and he holds my hand. When my expectations are not realized, there is still more of the story to unfold, and it will be better than any story I could write or hope for. There is more than I can see. I will not give up; my future is in God's hands.

§

No Prayer Today

Psalm 143:8 "Let me hear of your unfailing love each morning, for I am trusting you. Show me where to walk, for I give myself to you."

Psalm 5:3 "Listen to my voice in the morning, Lord. Each morning I bring my requests to you and wait expectantly."

Psalm 25:4-5 "Show me the right path, O Lord; point out the road for me to follow. Lead me by your truth and teach me, for you are the God who saves me. All day long I put my hope in you."

Jesus I know the fault is mine
so please forgive the wasted time
the empty days when prayer was passed
like glances in a looking glass
a glimmer all I saw of you
a faintly whispered word or two

If only I had stopped to pray
before I rushed into the day
I didn't listen to your voice
haphazardly I made my choice
and went where I'd no grace to be
then stayed put when you beckoned me

And all you planned to build with me
each step a walk in unity
is just a frayed unraveled heap
when night descends and I must sleep
with empty hands and muddled head
I lay exhausted on my bed

A hollow fruitless cloudy day
if I had taken time to pray
would I have found an anchor hold
a fence to keep me in the fold
a hand to steer me through the storm
a father's love to keep me warm

So often I neglect the one thing meant to give strength and definition to my day. I start with good intentions, but ordinary tasks waylay me and soon the morning is spent. I am flying out the door with a quickly breathed, "Help me, God." And that is it; my prayer for the day and I am on my own. I have not learned to dwell in the house of the Lord; I only rush through on my way to other places. There is a table spread with nourishment for my day, but I grab only a crust as I fly past. No time to sit still and eat now. My soul longs for the green pastures and still waters, but today I must run...no rest, no time, no prayer today.

§

LEAN HARD

Song of Solomon 8:5 "Who is this sweeping in from the desert leaning on her lover? ..."

2 Corinthians 12:8-10 "....'My grace is all you need. My power works best in weakness.' So now I am glad to boast about my weaknesses, so that the power of Christ can work through me. That's why I take pleasure in my weaknesses, and in the insults, hardships, persecutions, and troubles that I suffer for Christ. For when I am weak, then I am strong."

Psalm 139:10 "...your strength will support me."

Sometimes I don't want to lean
   I am an independent person
I can't always be
    running here and there
      with weaknesses flapping around me
     like unzipped sweaters
I wrap myself up tight
    belted and cinched
      with my own strength
I like to see how long
    I can stand up to adversity
   on my own
     near but separate
       precariously balanced on my own two feet
    until I fall
why can't I just say
     from the start
   I am a leaning person
    I was created to lean on God
     I must lean on God
God calls to me
   come closer
     you are not near enough
       not close enough for me to wrap my arms around you
not near enough to lean your head upon my chest

> Do you love me
>   then don't doubt me
>   but come
>   lean hard

I sometimes get into a perverse state of mind where, even though I know I am sinking, I don't want help from God. I desperately need help from God, but I hold off asking. I want to see if I can do this on my own. I roll around in self-pity, wrapped securely in inadequacy, waiting to see what will happen. The same thing always happens; I fail. Then, mercifully, God pulls me closer so I can lean on him again.

ॐ

WHEN GOD HIDES

Psalm 10:1 "O Lord, why do you stand so far away? Why do you hide when I am in trouble?"

God is in the shadows
watching over me
veiled within the darkness
where no one can see

I stand solitary
seemingly alone
but someone is watching
hidden and unknown

Though I feel abandoned
unseen and unheard
still someone is watching
but he speaks no word

What will I believe when
darkness hides his face
the lies that confuse me
and supplant his grace

A promise from the darkness
lifts my troubled heart
what can separate us
or keep us apart

I am always watching
I am always here
I am always faithful
there's no need to fear

I am in the shadows
watching over you
if the darkness hides me
still my eyes are true

What will I believe? Am I abandoned when God draws away into the darkness? God is greater than silence, bigger than darkness, stronger than loneliness, deeper than shadows, and higher than fear. He is faithful when all else fails. He keeps his promises in the darkness and in the silence. He is always there. He is always watching, always near, always present. I must choose to believe Him, and that is faith.

YOUR NAME IS NEAR

Psalm 75:1 "We thank you, O God! We give thanks because you are near..."

Psalm 119:151 "But you are near, O Lord, and all your commands are true."

Proverbs 18:10 "The name of the Lord is a strong fortress; the godly run to him and are safe."

Acts 4:12 "There is salvation in no one else! God has given no other name under heaven by which we must be saved."

Philippians 2:9-11 "...God elevated him to the place of highest honor and gave him the name above all other names, that at the name of Jesus every knee should bow, in heaven and on earth and under the earth, and every tongue declare that Jesus Christ is Lord, to the glory of God the Father."

Isaiah 51:1 "Listen to me all who hope for deliverance - all who seek the Lord! Consider the rock from which you were cut, the quarry from which you were mined."

> Your name is near
> hiding
> behind my eyes
> within my thoughts
> a heart beat
> the flutter of an eyelid
> away
> Your name is near
> with me
> name of the beloved
> name that calls to my name
> name of the deep
> name of the spaces above
> name of all that is hidden
> and all that can be seen
> Your name is near
> strong fortress
> hiding place
> the rock form which I am cut
> the quarry from which I am mined
> family name

name above all names
name that I call
    when my heart is overwhelmed
name that I breathe
    air in my lungs
name that brings me to my knees
blessed be
    your name

STAIRWAY TO HEAVEN

John 19:2-3 "The soldiers wove a crown of thorns and put it on his head, and they put a purple robe on him. 'Hail! King of the Jews!' they mocked, as they slapped him across the face."

Matthew 27:30-31 "And they spit on him and grabbed the stick and struck him on the head with it. When they were finally tired of mocking him, they took off the robe and put his own clothes on him again. Then they led him away to be crucified."

Luke 23:33-34 "When they came to a place called The Skull, they nailed him to the cross...Jesus said, 'Father, forgive them, for they don't know what they are doing...'"

Mark 15:33-34 and 37 "At noon darkness fell across the whole land until three o'clock. Then at three o'clock Jesus called out with a loud voice... 'My God, my God, why have you abandoned me?'...Then Jesus uttered another loud cry and breathed his last."

Romans 5:6-8 "When we were utterly helpless, Christ came at just the right time and died for us sinners. Now most people would not be willing to die for an upright person, though someone might perhaps be willing to die for a person who is especially good. But God showed his great love for us by sending Christ to die for us while we were still sinners."

They twisted together
a crown of thorns
and I was caught up
twisted together in that thorny branch
my sins were laid upon his head
my deeds drew his blood
I would like to think
that I am not responsible
I was years away
still hidden in time
how could he see me
who yet had no form and shape
no name
how could he have died for me
yet here I stand
I cannot walk around the cross
unless I pass through this gate

letting his innocent blood fall on me
      I have no path to the Father
my sins pierced his flesh
      my arrogance drew his blood
Christ, who knew no sin was made to be sin for me
      there is no other path
        there is no other stairway to heaven

GOD IN MY JOURNEY

THE JOURNEY

GOD IN MY JOURNEY

Proverbs 16:9 "We can make our plans, but the Lord determines our steps."

Proverbs 19:21 "You can make many plans, but the Lord's purpose will prevail."

I am on a journey through life. Sometimes it's a walk in the park, sometimes it's a roller-coaster ride. I make plans and preparations and set out with so many expectations of what things will look like and how the journey will proceed from beginning to end. But the best laid plans run amok. Life gallops off in directions I never anticipated while I am holding on for dear life and trying to figure out what I did wrong and why this is happening to me...

I get my breath. God's word begins to penetrate the confusion and speaks of other destinations and other plans...things I had never considered. The path has zigged when I thought it would zag, but it is still God's path and he still is laying out the steps for my feet. Hesitantly, I walk on. I must trust what I cannot see. My hope is not in the journey's end, but in the one who walks with me, leading the way.

I have relinquished my rights at the steering wheel. I'm not entirely sure where I will end up, but God is in the journey, and it will be the adventure of a lifetime...better than anything I cold have planned or imagined.

Psalm 119:105

"Your word is a lamp to guide my feet and a light for my path."

COMFORT HAD A DIFFERENT VOICE

Isaiah 55:8 "'My thoughts are nothing like your thoughts,' says the Lord. 'And my ways are far beyond anything you could imagine.'"

Isaiah 42:6 "I, the Lord, have called you to demonstrate my righteousness. I will take you by the hand and guard you..."

Isaiah 43:2-3 "When you go through deep waters, I will be with you. When you go through rivers of difficulty, you will not drown. When you walk through the fire of oppression, you will not be burned up; the flames will not consume you. For I am the Lord your God..."

You kept me safe within the storm
but in an unexpected form
I thought you'd come just like a lamb
to gently lead me home again

But you came roaring, full of teeth
and brought with you a taste of grief
you didn't hold and shelter me
but led me through the stormy sea

What I had planned, you brushed aside
you didn't turn back when I cried
the shore I came to, not my choice
and comfort had a different voice

But better than my best laid plan
You changed me when I held your hand
further I went than I could see
more I became than I could be

What I expect God to do and what God does are often two very different things. I embrace my expectations and anticipate my carefully thought out results. Then God comes in like a flood and everything is misplaced, rearranged, and washed away. I no longer recognize my life. When I cry and pout, God does not pity me and change the course he has ordained.

He takes my hand, and he begins to lead me through a landscape that I could not have envisioned on my own. Uncomfortable things buffet me, but God leads on. I want to stop, but God leads on. Darkness comes and I cannot see where I am going, but God leads on. Storms come and I long for shelter, but God leads on. The only thing that I do know is that he holds my hand. I begin to learn that faith has nothing to do with where I am going, but it rests in knowing and trusting the one who leads the way. And when the journey is done, I come to a place I never purposed to go, but where I always longed to be. I am a different person...better, more complete than I ever hoped to be. This was in God's mind all along, and I did not know and could not have planned for it. The only thing I could do was follow.

FLORA'S STORY

Psalm 121:1-8 "I look up to the mountains - does my help come from there? My help comes from the Lord, who made heaven and earth! He will not let you stumble; the one who watches over you will not slumber. Indeed, he who watches over Israel never slumbers or sleeps. The Lord himself watches over you! The Lord stands beside you as your protective shade. The sun will not harm you by day, nor the moon by night. The Lord keeps you from all harm and watches over your life. The Lord keeps watch over you as you come and go, both now and forever."

When I first met Flora she was 98 years old: a petite, white haired lady in a calico house dress. She was quiet, with a slow smile and hands folded demurely in her lap.

Ours was a slow-growing friendship of quiet visits and talks of our similar backgrounds growing up on farms, our shared faith in God...eventually we began to talk of deeper things. Life had not been easy for Flora. Her first husband died at an early age from the ravages of Tuberculosis. They had lived for a while in a tent in the Adirondack mountains because it was thought that exposure to the crisp, cold mountain air had healing qualities. She told once of coming up the mountain on her way home from teaching school. There had been steady snow all day and navigating the path on her snow-shoes had been an arduous task. Nearing their clearing, she suddenly realized their tent was no longer standing. She hurled herself on the pile of snow where the tent had been and with her bare hands dug her husband out of the snow. He had been trapped under his bed protected from the weight of the snow that had crushed the tent. He was chilled, but alive.

Having saved him once from the snow, she could not save him again from the disease that eventually took his life. She never fully recovered from the loss, but she did eventually remarry, having met a widower with small children. His children needed a mother, and she stepped in to fill that need.

Somewhere during the middle seasons of life, a darkness began to overtake her. Deeper and deeper she fell, until she could no longer reach the surface of life. In a near catatonic state, she was admitted to a psychiatric hospital, and there in a little room with one window, she waited. Every morning a nurse would get her out of bed, brush her hair and set her in a chair that faced the window. Every day she would stare out the window at the mountain ranges in the distance, unable to speak, unable to move, and unable to make a connection to life being lived around her.

But God, who had been her Savior from an early age, did not leave her alone in the darkness. Every day as she sat in the chair looking out the window at the mountains, she heard this verse repeated in her mind... "I look to the mountains - does my help come from there? My help comes from the Lord who made heaven and earth!" Every day the scripture repeated in her mind, and every day she rose a little closer to the light that called her. Miraculously, she made a full recovery and this is her testimony; the Word of God saved her when nothing else could. God spoke... God called her. His was the only voice that could penetrate the silence. He stood beside her; he watched over her...he pulled back the darkness and would not let the night steal her away. God called her back to the light.

SAFE IN THE WOODS

THE APPLE OF HIS EYE

Deuteronomy 32:10-11 "He found them in a desert land, in an empty, howling waste-land. He surrounded them and watched over them; he guarded them as he would guard his own eyes. Like an eagle that rouses her chicks and hovers over her young, so he spread his wings to take them up and carried them safely on his pinions."

Psalm 17:8 "Keep me as the apple of the eye, hide me under the shadow of thy wings." (KJV)

When I was a little girl I was lost in the woods. My father owned and operated a sugar bush, acres of old majestic maples that he tapped every spring to make maple syrup. I would often accompany him as he gathered the sap, following him as he rambled the length of the woods and back again...a path only he seemed to know with certainty.

On this particular day my father asked me to go with him, but I refused. Shortly after he left, I regretted my decision and wanted to be with him. The fact that I could no longer see him intensified my longing, and so I ran after him. On and on I ran until I could run no more, but my father was nowhere to be found. I have little memory of time passing, but I remember the feeling of tears running down my cheek, the icy wind, and the aloneness. I remember that my father did not come to hold me.

Much later, as darkness began to settle on the treetops, a man did find me. This man was not my father, but he gathered me up in his arms and he carried me home to my father. I was told later, it was the neighbor who found me. In my mad dash through the woods I had run clear across our property and halfway through his property. In the hundred plus acres of woods, it was a miracle that anyone found me. I do not remember much...but I will never forget the feeling of being carried home and the joy of being returned to my father's arms.

In revisiting this story, God gave me a new perspective. I had often thought of being lost and the joy of returning home to the father. I could always see God in this. But when God brought me back to this story, it was not the lost child that he focused on. This time, it was the neighbor who carried the child home to the father.

I always thought of the child as the apple of God's eye, the prized possession returned. But God began to speak to me about the neighbor, the man who had eyes to see the child who could not make it home to the father alone. "I will guard you because you must be my own eyes in a lost world. You must go out into the empty wastelands, but when you go I will watch over you, I will guard you like I guard my own eyes. You will see as I do; you will find the lost ones who can not find their own way, and you must carry them back to me. You are my eyes; I'm keeping you safe because you must see as I see. You are my eyes and my hands, and I will give you my heart."

I was once the lost child who needed to be carried home to the father. I longed to be with my father, but I did not know how to find him. Someone had to help me navigate the path through the woods, someone who knew the way, someone who knew my father. It is now my turn to see the lost children on the path around me. I must see with God's eyes and be willing to carry someone on that journey home. Not every lost child looks desperate, but with God's eyes, I will see the ones longing to find their father.

I LIVE TOO FAST

Ecclesiastes 9:11 "I returned and saw under the sun, that the race is not to the swift, nor the battle to the strong..." (KJV)

Psalm 39:6-7 "We are merely moving shadows, and all our busy rushing ends in nothing. We heap up wealth, not knowing who will spend it. And so, Lord, where do I put my hope? My only hope is in you."

Psalm 46:10 "Be still and know that I am God! ..."

I live too fast
   hurrying to accomplish things for which I have no reason
      extolling life in the fast lane
         as if vindicated by speed alone
      measuring my worth by the rate of achievement
but speed is a work of deception
   it puts a distance between me
      and the people I most love and want to be with
it counts on future destinations
      instead of enjoyment of the places already reached
   it embraces the thought that someday I will be able to give my
family the whole world
      instead of the moments
   when a kind word
      a game played
         a hug given
            would have meant the whole world and more
it saps my strength health and mental well being
      striving for a future
         I may never live to see
will this be my destiny
   that I out-ran all the ones
      who would have eased my loneliness and given me joy
         out-paced
            the grace allotted for each day
   out-distanced the treasures of moments

I can never live again
the memories that were meant to be cherished
for a lifetime

Sometimes I am snared by the acceleration of life that exchanges present joys for future successes. I think the speed with which I accomplish things justifies the sacrifices I exact from myself and my family. I live too fast.

Slow me down, God. Help me take time to make memories that will comfort and enrich my future and bring needed joy to the day at hand. Let me stop to embrace the people and the moments that I may never have again.

HIS MASTERPIECE

Ephesians 2:8-10 "God saved you by his grace when you believed. And you can't take credit for this; it is a gift from God. Salvation is not a reward for the good things we have done, so none of us can boast about it. For we are God's masterpiece. He created us anew in Christ Jesus, so we can do the good things he planned for us long ago."

Luke 15:24 "for this son of mine was dead and now has returned to life. He was lost, but now he is found..."

Psalm 111:9 "He has paid a full ransom for his people. He has guaranteed his covenant with them forever. What a holy, awe-inspiring name he has!"

The master carpenter took me
laid me out upon his knee
careful of the mangled parts and
gentle with the broken heart
returned was marked across my head
mechanisms all are dead
all movement gone, the paints worn bare
worthless and beyond repair

he looked at me with different eyes
saw some value, some lost prize
under the dirt, defaced and marred
he worked with hands also scarred
I felt he knew something of pain
cared to give me life again
would work until I was restored
without visible reward

he made me once again his own
the prodigal has come home
my life was lost but now is found
grave clothes round me all unbound
despite the sin that ravaged me
he paid a price, set me free
and he has chosen to forgive
I was dead, but now I live

We are created in Christ Jesus to do the good things he planned for us from the beginning of time. And we are twice his, owned by right of creation, his masterpiece, and owned by right of purchase, his ransomed treasure.

Nothing is broken beyond repair. The price has already been paid and the master carpenter waits. He alone has the skill to restore, the right to redeem and the love to search out his lost children and call them to come home.

BY REASON OF THIS BONDAGE

Exodus 2:23 "And it came to pass in process of time, that the king of Egypt died: and the children of Israel sighed by reason of the bondage, and they cried, and their cry came up unto God by reason of the bondage." (KJV)

John 16:33 "... Here on earth you will have many trials and sorrows. But take heart, because I have overcome the world."

Psalm 9:10 and 12 "Those who know your name trust in you, for you, O Lord, do not abandon those who search for you... He does not ignore the cries of those who suffer."

By reason of this bondage
the tongue that knew no prayer
found a reason to cry out
to see if God was there

By reason of this bondage
the hands so long hung down
have found a heavenward journey
lifted to touch God's crown

By reason of this bondage
the once unseeing eye
searches for the face of God
within the midnight sky

By reason of this bondage
imprisoning this heart
a greater journey I made
than ever I would start

If not for this great bondage
that causes me to be
reaching for the hand of God
and longing to be free

The things that teach me to search for God are not often pleasant things. Trouble, pain, sorrow, these things visit me. In the descending darkness, my spirit sighs by reason of the bondages I can not control or even understand. Need throws my arms up to reach for his hand. Desperation loosens my tongue, opens my eyes, and thaws my heart. I need him. I can not save myself, and that realization drives me into his arms. I need him. Even if I have been wayward and undeserving, as I am reaching up, God is reaching down. "Don't worry...I have you," He whispers. He holds my hand and leads me out of the wilderness. He lets me lean on him, as hard as I need to.

TOY SOLDIER

TIN SOLDIER

Psalm 71:3 "Be my rock of safety where I can always hide. Give the order to save me, for you are my rock and my fortress."

Psalm 23:5 "You prepare a feast for me in the presence of my enemies. You honor me by anointing my head with oil. My cup overflows with blessing."

Jeremiah 8:21-22 "I hurt with the hurt of my people. I mourn and am overcome with grief. Is there no medicine in Gilead? Is there no physician there? Why is there no healing for the wounds of my people?"

Come in out of the rain, out of the storm
come in
the Captain of the Lord's Army calls me to come in
but
I am a stiff tin soldier
with tin ears
determined to stand it out in the storm
determined to do it all by myself
not realizing how quickly I rust
in the slashing rains
inside his fortress
the Captain waits with oil
one anointing
would soften and free the joints
immobilized by the storm
the frozen heart
the rusty ear and eye
the stiff upper lip
the corroded hope
the oil waits
and I rust

I have a small, metal soldier in my china cabinet. He stands so resolute, so immovable...one arm crossed over his chest in salute, his eyes staring at some distant goal. He seems determined, unflinching, and unchanging, yet he is slowly rusting and corroding away. Already he has some fingers missing, and there are spots on his face eaten away by a leprosy of age. He does not seem to know his condition, but stands at tin soldier attention, as if he could go on forever.

I think I am sometimes like my steadfast tin soldier. I stand immovable in the storms of life determined to do it all by myself and prove to God I am a strong soldier. I don't cry out for help. I don't speak of my struggle or pain, but I stand as if nothing in the world could harm me. I am a soldier. I am on guard…I will not show weakness, need, weariness, grief or pain. I can do this alone.

God waits for me with the oil that would sooth the pain and bring strength and restoration. He is the strong fortress into which I can run; he has the medicine to heal my wounds…all that hinders me is my pride. I can not do this alone.

EVERY HEART HAS A SORROW

2 Corinthians 1:3-5 "...God is our merciful Father and the source of all comfort. He comforts us in all our troubles so that we can comfort others. When they are troubled, we will be able to give them the same comfort God has given us. For the more we suffer for Christ, the more God will shower us with his comfort through Christ."

My heart has a sorrow
and throbs with secret pain
a shadow passes over
sometimes a sudden rain

You can not see my secret
in day-to-day affairs
it hides behind my smile
but yet it's always there

I never speak the sorrow
behind its heavy lock
I only speak of safe things
when I am apt to talk

And yet it travels with me
and no one ever knows
but chains of bondage weight me
and heavier it grows

If you have known God's comfort
won't you speak to me
I'm drowning in this sorrow
that no one else can see

Please look a little deeper
and pray it might be clear
I'm crying out for help
in words no one can hear

> But God who knows my sorrow
> has set you in this place
> lead me to your Savior
> and help me see his face

Each one who knows Christ has something to offer. The same comfort I have received, I can give. It's easy to think that others don't need my kindness or my concern, but God calls me to look a little deeper and, by his grace, speak when he whispers in my ear. I can give a gift that could change a life forever.

BEE BALM

The Garden Must Grow Wild This Year

Proverbs 19:21 "You can make many plans, but the Lord's purpose will prevail."

Proverbs 16:9 "We can make our plans, but the Lord determines our steps."

Proverbs 16:1 "We can make our own plans, but the Lord gives the right answer."

> The garden must grow wild this year
> I have lost control of the dragonhead
> which has escaped the garden wall
> to run amok
> midst daisies who have no business
> being there
> I clamp my arms tight to my chest
> and still the urge to interfere
> I have fallen out of season
> the flowers do not care
> it would do them no good to explain
> and me no good in the telling
> the garden must grow wild this year
> I am no longer the author
> who writes the story
> it must weave its own destiny
> gallop wild to outcomes I can not control
> the garden must grow wild this year
> and I must learn
> in the waiting
> what was meant to live here

There is a four year cycle in a newly planted garden. The first year all life is sparse as new plants struggle to take hold and adjust to new conditions. All energy goes to the roots to ensure future survival. The second year, flowers are more plentiful and plants thrive. Energy will flow from the roots to nourish the plants. Improvements are obvious, but the garden has yet to reach its peak. The third year, all is at its best; growth is abundant and vibrant. This is the garden as it was envisioned when it was first planted. All the careful and exacting work of the gardener has come to fruition.

But the fourth year...somehow the fourth year...all things do not go as planned. Some plants will disappear altogether. Other plants will grow and bloom where they were never planted. Wildness creeps in and nature begins to declare itself uncontrollable. My best plans go awry, but yet there is undeniable beauty in the chaos. I am frustrated, and at the same time humbled, because I see that when my control dissipates, a greater voice emerges.

So it seems in life. When my fingerprints become too strong and squeeze the glory out of what God has called me to do, he disrupts my carefully laid plans. I am reminded that the outcomes were never mine to control. The garden must grow wild as I learn to relinquish my rights and let the garden become what God intended it to be.

GLOW IN THE DARK

Psalm 119:105 "Thy word is a lamp unto my feet and a light unto my path." (KJV)

Psalm 18:28 "You light a lamp for me. The Lord, my God, lights up my darkness."

Psalm 18:33 and 36 "He makes me as surefooted as a deer, enabling me to stand on mountain heights... You have made a wide path for my feet to keep them from slipping."

Hebrews 4:12 "For the word of God is alive and powerful. It is sharper than the sharpest two-edged sword, cutting between soul and spirit, between joint and marrow. It exposes our innermost thoughts and desires."

When I was a child I regularly attended Sunday School in a little white clapboard church in my town. My Mom was a Sunday School teacher, as were many of her friends, and Saturday night usually found her at the kitchen table cutting out crafts, Bible open in front of her as she prepared her lesson. Eventually I graduated into my Mom's class, but my first Sunday School teacher, a woman whose name I do not remember, was the one who God used to make a profound impact on my life.

This Sunday School teacher taught me as a young child to begin to memorize scripture. My first scripture was John 3:16, for which I received a small, silver colored medallion, with the verse printed on it, when I successfully said it from memory. It was the second scripture, however, for which I have the fondest memory. My teacher gave me a small wooden plaque with Psalm 119:105 printed on it with glow in the dark letters. At night, when I turned off the lights in my bedroom, there glowing at the foot of my bed were the words, "Thy word is a lamp unto my feet and a light unto my path." I can still see that plaque as it glowed night after night...the memory, and the verse, permanently etched in my mind.

When I was a teenager, and began to walk away from God...I remember sitting in a bus on my way to a city. When I was afraid, the words came unbidden to my mind..."Thy word is a lamp unto my feet and a light unto my path." And, the words not only repeated in my mind, but I saw them clearly in the luminescent green glow of that marvelous paint.

There were other moments of fear and uncertainty, when my Bible was gathering dust, unused on the shelf, that the green, glowing words would come to me. Always there was great comfort, like being brought back to childhood and the warmth and safety of my own bed. "Thy word is a lamp unto my feet and a light unto my path."

And so my journey, from childhood on, has been framed by those words that still glow in my mind. It was not the greenish, glow in the dark paint that kept those words alive in my heart. The living word of God kept calling me from the darkness...my signpost, the candle in the window, the word of God that lights up every darkness and calls every heart home. God would not let me forget that he had a path for my life and that he was the light that would help me find it.

His word was a lamp to my wayward feet and a beacon that guided me home.

THE DAY IS YOURS, AND YOURS ALSO THE NIGHT

Psalm 74:16-17 "Both day and night belong to you; you made the starlight and the sun. You set the boundaries of the earth, and you made both summer and winter."

Isaiah 45:7 "I create the light and make the darkness. I send good times and bad times. I, the Lord, am the one who does these things."

Job 2:10 "...Should we accept only good things from the hand of God and never anything bad?..."

Job 1:21 "...The Lord gave me what I had, and the Lord has taken it away. Praise the name of the Lord!"

Psalm 116:3-7 "Death wrapped its ropes around me; the terror of the grave overtook me. I saw only trouble and sorrow. Then I called on the name of the Lord: 'Please, Lord, save me!' How kind the Lord is! How good he is! So merciful, this God of ours! The Lord protects those of childlike faith; I was facing death and he saved me. Let my soul be at rest again, for the Lord has been good to me."

I move easily in the bright light of midday sun
    but in the pale glow
  of a less sure vision
    dim hopes wrapped in moonlight
     I pause
can this night also belong to God
  the intellect is quick to respond
    how could God let bad things happen to good people
     could a loving God really allow...
if I go down that road
    I must turn my back on all that God is
    and all that I know him to be
     I do not know why
  but the day is his
    and also the night
    I will be safe if I am with him

"Why, God...why?" Often the question cannot be answered in the moment it is asked. Like a tightly folded garment, it requires some unfolding and some ironing out before it can be worn with confidence. Will I give God time to help me in that process? Some things will stay hidden in the heart of God until the time he choses to reveal them, and there will be nothing I can do or say to change that.

The only thing that sets my soul at rest when night descends...when the winter is long...is knowing who my Father is. He hears my prayers and answers them... even when my voice is weak and my strength is spent, he bends down so that he can hear every word that I say. My Father is kind and good. He is merciful and he spreads his protection over me and hides me in his arms. If I know who God is, I am not so desperate to know why.

PRESSING IN

Luke 8:42-48 "... As Jesus went...he was surrounded by the crowds. A woman in the crowd had suffered for twelve years with constant bleeding, and she could find no cure. Coming up behind Jesus, she touched the fringe of his robe. Immediately, the bleeding stopped.

'Who touched me?' Jesus asked.

Everyone denied it, and Peter said, 'Master, this whole crowd is pressing up against you.'

But Jesus said, 'Someone deliberately touched me, for I felt healing power go out from me.' When the woman realized that she could not stay hidden, she began to tremble and fell to her knees in front of him. The whole crowd heard her explain why she had touched him and that she had been immediately healed. 'Daughter,' he said to her, 'your faith has made you well. Go in peace.'"

I cannot go another day
through jostling crowds I'll make a way
I must be heard so I cry out
I haven't time to stop and doubt
need throws all caution to the wind
and drives me to press after him
to find a place beside his feet
ignoring pain and dust and heat
I've lost all pride and self esteem
and need consumes my every dream
it sends me where I'd once not go
and urges me to not be slow
I stumble and I can not stand
but then his robe is in my hand
all I can do has come to this
to know his wrath or feel his kiss
he turns and with a touch of grace
lifts me to gaze into his face
then every need is met in him
though I just tried to touch his hem.

Great need is the catalyst that drives me into the arms of God. I can't wait for a better time. I can't walk; I have to run. And when I can not run I have to crawl. When there is no way I must force a way. All thoughts of looking good, maintaining my dignity, trying to earn or deserve his glance...all become meaningless in the face of my need. I have to touch God, there is no other help for me on earth or in heaven...only God. I am desperate, weak, falling, but my hand has found the edge of his robe and I hold on. And God reaches down to hold my hand. He lifts me to behold his face and says to me, "Your faith has made you well. Go in peace."

WITH EYES SHUT TIGHT

Proverbs 4:25-26 "Look straight ahead, and fix your eyes on what lies before you. Mark out a straight path for your feet; stay on the safe path."

Proverbs 20:24 "The Lord directs our steps, so why try to understand everything along the way?"

Sometimes
    I shut my eyes
        and ask the Lord to lead me
when I should
    open my eyes wide
        and use the sight
    already given
        to walk the path
    already made straight before me
but I am reluctant
        to begin
with eyes shut tight
    I pray for another sign
    some special miracle to seal the journey
        beyond any shadow of doubt
but God says
    open your eyes
        there is a time to pray
    with eyes shut tight
        and a time to walk
    with eyes wide open
you were given eyes for a reason

I sometimes hide behind prayer, disguising my reluctance to follow as a pious wish to be absolutely certain of where I am going. Prayer is always the first step of any journey, but sometimes I pray...and pray...and pray...and pray. I keep squeezing my eyes shut, hoping if I delay long enough I may miraculously get to the finish line before I start the journey.

There are seasons of waiting, and seasons of standing absolutely still. But sometimes the path is clear before me and God is waiting for me to open my eyes and walk with him on the path made plain before my feet. "Open your eyes," He says, "And walk with the sight I gave you. Look straight ahead, and follow me."

TULIPS IN THE SNOW

COME AWAY WITH ME

Mark 6:31 "Then Jesus said, 'Let's go off by ourselves to a quiet place and rest awhile...'"

Song of Solomon 2:10-13 "My lover said to me, 'Rise up, my darling! Come away with me, my fair one! Look, the winter is past, and the rains are over and gone. The flowers are springing up, the season of singing birds has come, and the cooing of turtledoves fills the air. The fig trees are forming young fruit, and the fragrant grapevines are blossoming. Rise up, my darling! Come away with me, my fair one!'"

> Come away with me
> I will heal what you cannot heal
> I will set free what you cannot
> I will interrupt your routine
> You don't need to understand
> just come

I have learned that sometimes God interrupts my routine in ways that would not be my choice. Sometimes it is sickness. I am home...unsettled, unwell, out of balance. I don't feel like going away to a quiet place with God. I would like to feel sorry for myself, and go to bed with a cup of hot tea.

But God says, "Come away."

In that call there is more than just the expectation that I will sit down with my Bible and try to read a little if I should feel like it. It is the call to pay attention. It is the call to listen, to be quiet on the outside until the cacophony on the inside is also soothed and stilled.

To "come away" is not a call for cowards. I do not want to be still because it means being alone in a vulnerable place with nothing to interrupt God's purpose and intention. It is laying aside distraction and every avoidance technique; it is taking the barricades from around my heart and letting God walk in with no restrictions. It takes time. I am so layered with protections, like a child going out to play on a cold January morning. I have mittens, ear muffs, layers of sweaters, scarves and coats, boots, wool socks; I am ready to not be touched by the world around me.

But God says, "Come away."

The winter is past, he tells me. You have accumulated too much around your life, insulating yourself against intimacy with me. But the flowers are springing up, the season of singing birds has come. It is time to unwrap, declutter and strip away to expose again the softness of your spirit to the gentle breath of the Holy Spirit. Rise up…come away.

And when I come away, God unwraps, layer by layer, the things that have come between us. It must happen in the time of rest, the time of uninterrupted aloneness. It is what we will not do unless we are hidden away where no one else watches us but God. In these moments God not only penetrates my defenses, but he also heals what I cannot. He sets free the things I cannot.

When God says "Come away," it may feel like an unwanted bump in my road, but it is essential. I may not understand, but I must go.

WE HANGED OUR HARPS ON THE WILLOWS

Psalms 137:1-4 "By the rivers of Babylon, there we sat down, yea, we wept, when we remembered Zion. We hanged out harps upon the willows in the midst thereof. For there they that carried us away captive required of us a song; and they that wasted us required of us mirth, saying, sing us one of the songs of Zion. How shall we sing the Lord's songs in a strange land?" (KJV)

Habakkuk 3:17-18 "Even though the fig trees have no blossoms, and there are no grapes on the vines; even though the olive crop fails, and the fields lie empty and barren; even though the flocks die in the fields, and the cattle barns are empty, yet I will rejoice in the Lord! I will be joyful in the God of my salvation!"

I have a friend who composed a haunting ballad based on Psalm 137:1-4. She sang the song for those who had hung their harps on the willows and could sing no more... She sang the words of hopelessness, but the very melody lifted the hearer beyond that moment to healing and restoration. When feelings say, "it is time to hang my harp on the willows. I can't go beyond this river of confusion." The song says, "This may be how I feel at the moment, but my harp is in my hand and I am singing my heart to the Lord. Even if it is a song of sorrow, he will hear me, he will help me." It is the paradox of singing the song that says, "I can sing no more." The very act defies the intent and takes me to a victory I could not win on my own. I sat down by the rivers of Babylon, the rivers of confusion, and I wept, but I never hung my harp on the willows. I didn't silence my song to the Lord. I sang the Lord's song in a strange and desolate land and he heard me and he was suddenly there with me.

Sometimes hard things happen in life; there are no blossoms on the trees and no grapes on the vine...no spring, no fruit, no hope. Sometimes it all fails and life becomes unbearably empty and barren. I feel reduced to nothing. Sometimes death comes and a house is empty long before its time.

I have a choice, as I sit down by this river of confusion and weep on its banks. I can hang my harp on the willows. Or, I can cling to my harp and choose to sing the Lord's song in this strange land. The enemy will taunt me, as he comes to carry me away captive in my grief. "How can you sing the Lord's song in a strange land? How can you even think about rejoicing?"

Yet I must rejoice in the Lord, in the God of my salvation. I can not leave my harp and my song in this place, for if I do then I go forward into captivity. Even if I begin with the song that says, "God, I can not sing...," I must pour it all out to

God. I can tell him what has happened. It is all right to say, "It's all gone, there is no blossom, no fruit..." But I must end with, "Yet I will rejoice in the Lord... God, I'm here with my tears and my harp... I'm not going to let go of you...I'm going to trust you...I'm going to give you my song in the night hours...but you must bring the morning's light."

STAINED GLASS

Isaiah 61:3 "To all who mourn in Israel, he will give a crown of beauty for ashes, a joyous blessing instead of mourning, festive praise instead of despair. In their righteousness, they will be like great oaks that the Lord has planted for his own glory."

Psalm 147:3 "He heals the brokenhearted and bandages their wounds."

The particular beauty
of stained glass
is that it was first broken
then
pieced together again
in exquisite patterns
fragments
redeemed
the untrained eye
sees
only a pile
of brokenness
stained colors
without sense or order
God sees the finished work
restored
built together again
by his hands
myriad of hues
reflecting lights
shadows
shades
of His glory
the greatest beauty
wrested
from brokenness
shinning joy
instead of ashes

Many things in life can break us into pieces, but only God can take those pieces and fashion a work of intricate beauty and artistry. He redeems the pieces scattered in disarray across the floor; muddied, raw and fragmented beyond repair. He holds them gently in his hand and does not despise or reject what they have become. He has vision beyond the brokenness; he sees the marvelous window that is in his heart to create. He binds up the wounds of brokenness, forgives the stain of sin and heals the jagged edges of separation. In his hands, a wonderful work emerges...beauty for ashes, joyous blessing instead of mourning, and praise instead of despair.

His work is completed when the light of his presence radiates through the once shattered glass, transforming brokenness into heavenly splendor.

DADDY IS A BIG, BIG MAN

Deuteronomy 32:11 "Like an eagle that rouses her chicks and hovers over her young, so he spreads his wings to take them up and carried them safely on his pinions."

Isaiah 40:11 "He will feed his flock like a shepherd. He will carry the lambs in his arms, holding them close to his heart. He will gently lead the mother sheep with their young."

Psalms 28:9 "... Lead them like a shepherd, and carry them in your arms forever."

Isaiah 46:3-4 "... I have cared for you since you were born. Yes, I carried you before you were born. I will be your God throughout your lifetime - until your hair is white with age. I made you, and I will carry you along and save you."

When my son was two years old, we were enjoying a family picnic in the country. Our flannel blanket was spread under the boughs of a huge maple tree, and after our lunch of sandwiches and fresh pears, we walked together down a narrow dirt road to the river. My son walked between us, one hand holding his Daddy's hand and the other hand snuggly in mine.

After enjoying the beauty of the river from the wood-planked bridge, we turned around and started back. But, my little boy's strength had given out, his little legs exhausted. My husband swung him up on his shoulders and carried him the rest of the way. With his little hands securely clasped on my husband's forehead he sang a song to the rhythm of the long, sure strides... "Daddy is a big, big man... Daddy is a big, big man..."

When my own strength gives out and my walk falters, there is someone who lifts me up and carries me. He never questions why I cannot keep going on my own, or tells me I am too old for his help. He carries me, even when my hair has turned white with age...he carries me. He swings me up on his shoulders and from that height, my hands on his forehead and my feet swinging in space, my perspective changes.

From this vantage point, my problems seem far away and my strength and power feel infinite. It is no longer my own strength, but the strength of the one who carries me and the power of his long, sure strides that propels me forward. He is bigger than all my problems, he is larger than every word shouted against me, he is stronger than the tide of events threatening to overpower me...I no longer have to navigate or figure it all out. For this moment in time when my strength is gone, he carries me. I am not shipwrecked; I am not stalled by the side of the road...I am moving forward faster than I could have traveled on my own and there is a deep joy that rises in that journey. I can kick out my weary feet and spread my bruised toes in rest because my father carries me and I am safe. A song rises in my heart also... "My Daddy is a big, big man."

THE GREATEST INVASION

Isaiah 9:6-7 "For unto us a child is born, unto us a son is given: and the government shall be upon his shoulder: and his name shall be called Wonderful, Counselor, the mighty God, the everlasting Father, the Prince of Peace. Of the increase of his government and peace there shall be no end, upon the throne of David, and upon his kingdom, to order it, and to establish it with judgment and with justice form henceforth even forever. The zeal of The Lord of hosts will perform this." (KJV)

Luke 11:2 "... Thy kingdom come, thy will be done, as in heaven, so in earth." (KJV)

> The greatest invasion
> the earth ever knew
> was quietly witnessed
> by only a few
>
> the mightiest war cry
> came hidden within
> the cry of a baby
> born without sin
>
> the humblest beginnings
> no throne and no ring
> the beasts of the stable
> attended their king
>
> the captain of legions
> lay down in the hay
> and the richest of kings
> had no crown that day
>
> but the darkness was pierced
> a shaft of pure light
> ignited the world on
> that glorious night

all eternity changed
by the coming of one
the greatest invasion
the birth of God's son

Forever changed. I am forever changed by that day, by the coming of my Savior. Everything I know of life hinges on that moment in history. Every step of my journey is routed through that humble stable in Bethlehem.

The world, and everything in it, changed forever with the quiet, simple invasion of one child...the light born to conquer the darkness...Emmanuel, God with us.

FROM BEHIND THE GLASS

NOW WE SEE THROUGH A GLASS, DARKLY

I Corinthians 13:12 "Now we see things imperfectly, like puzzling reflections in a mirror, but then we will see everything with perfect clarity. All that I know now is partial and incomplete, but then I will know everything completely, just as God now knows me completely."

I Corinthians 13:12 "For now we see through a glass, darkly; but then face to face: now I know in part; but then shall I know even as also I am known." (KJV)

Proverbs 20:12 "Ears to hear and eyes to see - both are gifts from the Lord."

When I was recovering from eye surgery, I saw everything through a bubble that had been inserted in my eye to hold the retina in place. The world took on a wavy, under-water effect and all things, although recognizable, were distorted. There was a slight juxtaposition of obstacles, so that when I thought I was pouring coffee into my mug, instead I poured it on the counter. When I reached for something, I often missed by just a fraction of an inch. Light reflections danced around the bubble with strobe-like effects. In short, my perspective changed. I began to see through a glass darkly; objects became puzzling reflections. Life was recognizable, but lacked clarity.

The longer I lived with my "bubble" the more normal it seemed. I got used to it and learned to make the minor adjustments necessary to compensate for the irregularities of vision. It soon became possible to think, "this is normal…I'm seeing all there is to see." I no longer consciously looked through a bubble…through a glass, darkly. I accepted limitation as life, and was content.

Physically, the bubble in my eye slowly dissipated and in a matter of a few months I no longer had distorted vision. But even with clearer physical vision, all that I see is still partial and incomplete. I cannot see the depths of the spiritual realm inhabited by God. I catch a glimpse, a reflection here…a shadow there, but I cannot see it clearly. There is more. How easy it is to accept limitations and to think that I see all that God is doing.

I remember the sensations of getting eyeglasses for the first time. How amazed I was to discover that trees had sharp, clearly defined twigs and branches that could be seen from a distance. Reality shifted to a new dimension…one that I did not consider until I began to wear corrective lenses.

So it will be someday. Reality will shift to a new dimension, and I will one day see with perfect clarity. In that day I will know everything completely, just as God knows me completely. Until that time, God help me to remember that I cannot see all that you are doing in my life and in the lives of those around me. For the eyes you have given me, I thank you. What an incredible gift! But for all that I cannot see, and for all that I will one day see, I also thank you. Now I know in part, but then shall I know even as also I am known.

JONAH

Jonah 1:3 "But Jonah got up and went in the opposite direction to get away from the Lord..."

Jonah 2:5-6 "I sank beneath the waves, and the waters closed over me. Seaweed wrapped itself around my head. I sank down to the very roots of the mountains. I was imprisoned in the earth, whose gates lock shut forever. But you, O Lord my God, snatched me from the jaws of death!"

Deep in the hole of rebellion
my blanket over my head
I hoped that God would not find me
rattle me out of my bed

thrown into the ocean's depths
I sank to the heart of the sea
down to the roots of the mountains
great billows washed over me

God ran in the thunderous waves
caught me in the raging storm
tied me up tight in his seaweed
bedraggled wet and forlorn

into the fishes belly
deposited me on my knees
my valley of decision
in the depths of the tossing seas

he found me in my rebellion
wrestled me over my fate
when at last I could surrender
he unlocked my prison gate

Sometimes my journey is not towards God, but away from God. I hate to admit it, but I have my moments of obstinate rebellion. Like Jonah, I know what it's like to hide deep inside a home…a vessel…and pull the blankets over my head. I hope to hide from the things I do not want to face.

But God will not leave me alone. He will find me…he has promised to always find me, even in my rebellion when I do not want to be found. He restrains me with the truth of his word until I can relax the tightness of my will and begin to hear the direction that brings life and peace. When I can finally surrender, I find myself no longer in the prison of my own making, but in a place of great freedom and usefulness…the place of his making.

KINGS GO OUT TO WAR

Revelation 5:10 "And has made us unto our God kings and priests: and we shall reign on the earth." (KJV)

Psalm 144:1 "Praise the Lord, who is my rock. He trains my hands for war and gives my fingers skill for battle."

Isaiah 45:5 "I am the Lord; there is no other God. I have equipped you for battle..."

Ephesians 6:10-13 "...Be strong in the Lord and in his mighty power. Put on all of God's armor so that you will be able to stand firm against all the strategies of the devil. For we are not fighting against flesh-and-blood enemies, but against evil rulers and authorities of the unseen world, against mighty powers in this dark world, and against evil spirits in the heavenly places. Therefore, put on every piece of God's armor so you will be able to resist the enemy in the time of evil. Then after the battle you will still be standing firm."

Trumpets sound the cry
Banners fill the sky
Faces set like flint
Holy armors glint
Fierce and valiant men
Vision clothing them
Swords are at their sides
Holy Spirit guides
Fires burn within
Destiny to win
Settling the score
Kings go out to war

I am a king unto my God, and kings go out to war. Sometimes it takes me a little while to remember this. My mirror reminds me daily that I no longer have physical youth and strength. The enemy taunts, "You're no warrior! You'd better sit down before you get hurt. Who do you think you are?"

But I know who I am. I may not look anything like a king or a warrior, but underneath this cloak of ordinary humanity, there is a hidden armor waiting and a sharp and deadly sword resting. When battle lines are drawn and my territory is threatened by the enemy, I cast aside what can be seen and stand clothed in the armor of God and armed with the sword of the spirit. God has equipped me to do battle and he has trained my hands for war. It doesn't matter what I look like on the outside, inside I am a warrior.

I wrap my hand around the hilt of my sword, the word of God. I will not only resist, but I will stand firm and be strong in the Lord and in his mighty power. The victory is the Lord's, but he has chosen me to stand as a warrior so that I might share with him the thrill of triumph.

THE WORD OF TRUTH

John 17:17 "Make them holy by your truth; teach them your word, which is truth."

Psalm 86:11 "Teach me your ways, O Lord, that I may live according to your truth! Grant me purity of heart so that I may honor you."

John 14:6 "Jesus told him, 'I am the way, the truth, and the life. No one can come to the Father except through me."

John 8:44 "For you are the children of your father the devil, and you love to do the evil things he does. He was a murderer from the beginning. He has always hated the truth, because there is no truth in him. When he lies, it is consistent with his character; for he is a liar and the father of lies."

> Satan's lies
> deceiving eyes
> firebrand tongue
> decaying lung
> putrid breath
> the stench of death
> unholy guise
> Satan's lies

There was a morning when all I could hear was whispered fear, the murmurs of long ago wounds, repetitions of all my faults, crushing words of failure...like a storm these words cycled around me. I began to doubt myself and my relationship with God; all that I had thought good in life shook under accusations of weakness and worthlessness.

In that torrent of words, I managed one small prayer, "Lord, I can no longer distinguish truth from lies. Please, God, silence every voice that shouts against me that is not the voice of your Holy Spirit."

Silence. In a matter of moments...silence. I took a deep breath; letting peace fill me. It was a dramatic answer to my desperate prayer. Why had I never prayed like this before? I have certainly heard the voices before; they come in my weakest moments, spiraling me down to the place where emotions overwhelm clear thought. They rob me of joy, bring anxiety over things I can not change, and worry for the future I cannot control.

They are voices that do not speak truth, but they shout so loudly that they take the driver's seat, and I abdicate under their persistent barrage. I am overwhelmed by lies that seem so true. But there is a voice that speaks truth, the voice of the Holy Spirit. His still, small voice resonates under the shouts of the enemy…waiting for me to hear. When I tune my ear to his voice, the lies that pull strength from darkness are revealed in light and I can see them for what they are. God has a much different story to tell me; his words are strength and life and he speaks hope for the future and release from the past that he has already forgiven and will not remember…and neither should I.

I can make a choice. I can decide each day which voice I will listen to, which voice will speak into my day, which voice will direct my steps. The voice of truth is waiting.

WHAT STANDS BEHIND

A WORD BEHIND YOU

Isaiah 30:21 "Your own ears will hear him. Right behind you a voice will say, 'This is the way you should go,' whether to the right or to the left."

Psalm 23:4 "Even when I walk through the darkest valley, I will not be afraid, for you are close beside me. Your rod and your staff protect and comfort me."

Psalm 18:28 "You light a lamp for me. The Lord, my God, lights up my darkness."

Psalm 119:105 "Your word is a lamp to guide my feet and a light for my path."

I'm afraid, darkness has hidden the view
fear not I am standing right behind you
I don't see you, Lord, are you really here
I am behind you, have nothing to fear
but what if I stumble, what if I fall
I am behind you to hear if you call
and if Satan should come what will he see
he'll look behind you and only see me

Sometimes inspiration stands behind me, not in front of me. I am accustomed to looking ahead, setting a goal and running towards it. I want a clear view of the future, and a wide open path. But, sometimes there is nothing in front of me but darkness and uncertainty. How can I walk forward blindly in the night?

Then the wind comes gently from behind and begins to fill the sails. A word comes from behind and says this is the way, walk in it...trust me. It does not change the fact that darkness looms before me and the path is treacherous. It doesn't remove the enemy lurking along the way. It doesn't reveal the God that I can not see, but the word behind me teaches me the places to set my feet so that I can walk in safety. And even though I may feel that I face the enemy alone, in the moments of confrontation there is one who rises up behind me to fight on my behalf. He is the one who draws the enemy's eyes away from me, mighty and powerful in his glory. I do not see him, but he is the light behind me that pierces my darkness, and the word that rescues me.

ORDINARY REFLECTING DIVINE

2 Corinthians 4:7 "We now have this light shining in our hearts, but we ourselves are like fragile clay jars containing this great treasure. This makes it clear that our great power is from God, not ourselves."

I came into the kitchen last night
laundry basket in hand
to find
the glass dome off the butter dish
dirty knife beside it
reflecting mutely
the soft colored lights

unexpected beauty
ordinary
reflecting divine

We have this treasure in clay jars, but even clay jars have moments of great beauty when they transcend the earth they were made from and touch heaven. The light of God's love shines out of earthly eyes; the colors of heaven escape for a moment and radiate from a life bound to earth, but reaching for heaven.

Suddenly, in the midst of my ordinary, messy life, there is a spark of glory ignited and God shines out like a candle newly lit. It changes everything. Ordinary reflecting divine. No longer ordinary, I see God in my kitchen, in the middle of my life, in the center of things not perfect and not cleaned up, and not made ready for him...but there he is. He comes and brings unexpected beauty and joy. He makes my heart sing a song that I did not know was waiting.

I have this light shining in my heart, but I am like a fragile clay jar containing this treasure. The miracle of the shining is that God came in and touched the clay, the ordinary, with the divine light of his glory and power. It was his choice, not mine...and he came.

AFTER WORDS

ABOUT THE AUTHOR

Ellen Mainville lives in northern New York, in a Victorian house with abundant flower gardens. She is a teacher, artist, and writer who has worked for many years in public and private schools in the area. Her husband, Mark, is an Associate Pastor of a local church. They have been married for more than thirty years.

Ellen has two sons, Nate and Andrew, both living and working on the west coast. Nate, in the military, is often found creating things in his well-equipped garage. Nate and Heather have a family of five. Ellen and Mark greatly look forward to and enjoy time spent with children and grand-children. Andrew works in Washington state, where he too is a writer and artist. He is also an accomplished photographer: the cover photograph and author's picture are Andrew's handiwork. Danielle, who lives with Ellen and Mark, is the "daughter they always wanted…and now have." She is a great joy and adds a lot of life to their old Victorian house. Coco, the Standard Poodle, is another treasured family member.

Besides teaching, writing, and her art, Ellen also enjoys gardening, sewing, and reading. She is an active leader in her church, especially in the areas of mentoring and teaching.

CPSIA information can be obtained
at www.ICGtesting.com
Printed in the USA
FSOW03n0512281017
40310FS